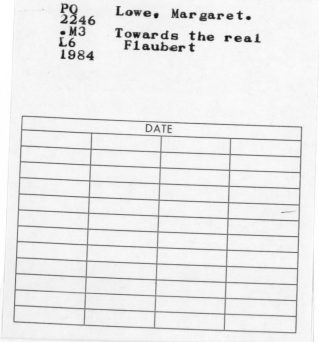

Towards the Real Flaubert

Towards the Real Flaubert

A Study of 'Madame Bovary'

MARGARET LOWE

Edited, with a foreword and a postface,
by A. W. Raitt

CLARENDON PRESS · OXFORD
1984

Oxford University Press, Walton Street, Oxford OX2 6DP
London New York Toronto
Delhi Bombay Calcutta Madras Karachi
Kuala Lumpur Singapore Hong Kong Tokyo
Nairobi Dar es Salaam Cape Town
Melbourne Auckland
and associated companies in
Beirut Berlin Ibadan Mexico City Nicosia

Published in United States
by Oxford University Press, New York

British Library Cataloguing in Publication Data
Lowe, Margaret
Towards the real Flaubert.
1. Flaubert, Gustave. Madame Bovary
I. Title II. Raitt, A.W.
843'.8 PQ2246.M3
ISBN 0-19-815800-9

Library of Congress Cataloging in Publication Data
Lowe, Margaret.
Towards the real Flaubert.
Bibliography: p.
Includes index.
1. Flaubert, Gustave, 1821–1880. Madame Bovary.
I. Raitt, A. W. (Alan William) II. Flaubert, Gustave,
1821–1880. Madame Bovary. III. Title.
PQ2246.M3L6 1984 843'.8 84-14898
ISBN 0-19-815800-9

Typeset by Cotswold Typesetting Ltd, Cheltenham
Printed in Great Britain by
Biddles Ltd, Guildford

Foreword

On 14 November 1850, Flaubert wrote to Louis Bouilhet that one of the subjects he was contemplating for his next novel was the story of 'la jeune fille qui meurt vierge et mystique, entre son père et sa mère, dans une petite ville de province, au fond d'un jardin planté de choux et de quenouilles, au bord d'une rivière grande comme l'Eau de Robec'. It is generally recognized, despite the obvious differences, that this represents the first germ of the idea for *Madame Bovary*. But in the same letter Flaubert mentions two other subjects he has in mind: 'j'en ai trois, qui ne sont peut-être que le même et ça m'emmerde considérablement.' The two other subjects are *Une nuit de Don Juan* and 'l'histoire d'*Anubis*, la femme qui veut se faire baiser par le Dieu'. That Flaubert could identify the subject which was to evolve into *Madame Bovary* with one that dealt expressly with myth shows that he was well aware of a mythological dimension to his inspiration, a dimension hardly surprising in view of the immense study of myths he had undertaken for *La Tentation de saint Antoine*. It is of course obvious that *Salammbô* is shot through with mythological elements, some overt, others less apparent, and these have been thoroughly examined in recent years, notably by Anne Green in *Flaubert and the Historical Novel: 'Salammbô' Reassessed* (Cambridge, 1982). But, so far, no one has attempted a systematic investigation of the way in which the mythological dimension affected those other novels by Flaubert in which its presence is not openly proclaimed.

This was the field in which Margaret Lowe was working, and the series of articles which she had published over the years, especially on *Madame Bovary* and *Hérodias*, had strikingly demonstrated how original and how fruitful her approach was. All Flaubert specialists were thus eagerly awaiting the full-scale book on the subject which she was known to be writing. Sadly, when she died suddenly in Paris in November 1982, the work was still not finished. But the greater part of it was ready to be sent to the publisher, and, since that part is complete in itself and can be read independently of anything else, it has seemed right to make it available to those many people who had been looking forward to the appearance of the book.

In a note to the last article she wrote, "'Rendre plastique . . .'": Flaubert's Treatment of the Female Principle in *Hérodias*, post-humously published in the *Modern Language Review* in July 1983, Margaret Lowe had announced her forthcoming book under the title *Masculine Feminine: Towards the Real Flaubert.* Her intention was to provide a detailed study of *Madame Bovary*, and then, much more briefly, to consider some of the ramifications of the theme in the later novels, ending with a conclusion in which she would have given a synthesis of her findings and justified her title. At the time of her death, the section on *Madame Bovary* was finished, part of a chapter on *Salammbô* had been sketched out, but the remainder existed only in note form. It is consequently the study of *Madame Bovary* which is presented here, and, while everyone will regret that she did not live to round off the book as she would have wished, it is clear that what she has written on *Madame Bovary* constitutes an autonomous whole which is of profound interest to all concerned with that inexhaustible novel and indeed with Flaubert in general. Her proposed title has been slightly modified to take account of this.

A word of explanation is called for on the form of the present publication. Not all it contains had reached quite the same stage when Margaret Lowe died. The preface and the first four chapters had been typed and corrected by the author; the fifth and sixth chapters were still in manuscript, virtually definitive but with one or two gaps and one or two sections not fully written up. Fortunately, it has been possible to make good these lacunae from earlier drafts or previous publications, except that Chapter Six ends abruptly, with-out the tailpiece Dr Lowe intended to add; this would however not have occupied more than a few pages, and the argument is un-affected.

The main text is thus very much as Dr Lowe desired. On the other hand, the notes still remained to be written, and these have had to be added. They consist very largely of references to quotations and to secondary literature; it would have been presumptuous to go beyond that. It did not appear necessary to supply page references for the very numerous quotations from *Madame Bovary* itself: the vast majority of them will be familiar to every reader of the novel, and any that are not can easily be located through the *Concordance to Flaubert's 'Madame Bovary'* by Charles Carlut, Pierre H. Dubé, and

J. Raymond Dugan (New York and London, Garland, 1978). For the works by Flaubert and for his correspondence, the edition used is that of the *Œuvres complètes* published by the Club de l'Honnête Homme in Paris between 1971 and 1976, which is at present the most complete if not the most reliable. A small number of quotations from the letters have resisted all attempts at identification, despite the expert and willing help of D. A. Williams and Dr Adrianne Tooke, but for the most part they consist only of a few words and are not of great significance. It has also been impossible to furnish references for some of the quotations from authors other than Flaubert, notably from Creuzer's enormous compilation *Les Religions de l'antiquité*, where the sheer size of the work would have rendered any search futile.

Margaret Lowe was a remarkable woman and a remarkable scholar, and she is deeply mourned by her many friends round the world. It will be some consolation to them that this book, to which she devoted so much energy, intelligence, and sensitivity, can stand as a memorial to her.

A. W. RAITT

Contents

Preface

The object of this study is to demonstrate that Flaubert the peerless and accurate portrayer of his own period and his own contemporaries is also an allegorical and symbolist writer, bent upon placing these modern works against a wider historical and, eventually, cosmic background. By the same criteria, those of his works set in ancient societies, evoking the manners and religions of antiquity, have still as their aim to illustrate his own epoch.

Flaubert's method is that of the *troubadour* he called himself, that is, the finder and re-teller of traditional tales. Behind each work we glimpse as substructure one major and many other ancillary literary and mythical themes or legends such as the poets—Classical, Romantic, 'Orphic' ('car c'est tout un')[1]—have chosen immemorially for their power of evocation and their universal significance. This is true of *Madame Bovary, Salammbô, L'Éducation sentimentale,* the *Trois Contes, Bouvard et Pécuchet.* 'Le Moderne, l'Antique, le Moyen Âge—subtilités de rhéteur, voilà mon opinion!'[2] Flaubert declared late in life, and all his works, in whatever setting he has placed them, illustrate a theme already clearly stated in *Madame Bovary:* 'l'éternelle monotonie de la passion, qui a toujours les mêmes formes et le même langage'—all the passions, not just the passion of love.

What of the techniques used by writers in these epochs? Again, in his generalizing intention, Flaubert adopts and adapts many of them. *Madame Bovary* is a modern tale told with the 'procédés des anciens'[3] (that is, emphasizing irony and fatality); in *Salammbô,* Flaubert wishes to 'fixer un mirage en appliquant à l'antiquité les procédés du roman moderne',[4] with the result that readers of his own time and ours exclaim in horror at the 'realism' of his battle scenes. *L'Éducation sentimentale* is a quest told in medieval manner, recalling Dante, the Romance of the Rose, and the *roman d'aventures* which Flaubert had always wanted to write. *La Tentation de saint Antoine* takes the form of a mystery play; *Bouvard et Pécuchet* is an Odyssey transposed into the modern world; the *Trois Contes,* three versions of the lives of Christian saints, recall also his once avowed intention of writing a 'conte oriental'.[5]

Each of Flaubert's works is an *allegory* in the most general sense, a variation on the theme of Psyche and Eros. Each is a *myth* in itself, that is, a variation on the theme of man and nature. Each is also a meditation on the theme of the artist, on the Apollonian as opposed to the Dionysiac, so that, in each, Orpheus, that figure beloved of nineteenth-century France, is discernible. The Dance of Death, the *Götterdämmerung*, the historical evolution of the archetypal concepts of masculine and feminine, the mystic marriage of heaven and earth, the dialectic between sun and moon, between Hercules and Isis, are shown to be interwoven into the texture of the works, producing the complexity, profundity and impetus that characterize them. The rules that govern societies, ancient and modern, emerge and are mutually illuminating. Above all, religion, from which 'les moeurs dérivent',[6] stands out in all its paramount importance. Its continuity, in particular, is stressed, especially in *La Tentation de saint Antoine*. Flaubert's works thus provide repeated examples of how in a time of totalitarianism and censorship it is possible by means of the ancient techniques of allegory and symbolism to pinpoint characteristics of the present and to expose them, while at the same time never losing sight of the 'côtés immuables de l'âme',[7] of the primitive consciousness, the study of which, in his battle against 'l'éternelle Blague',[8] was Flaubert's abiding preoccupation. 'L'humanité est ainsi, il ne s'agit pas de la changer, mais de la connaître.'[9]

CHAPTER ONE

Prolegomena

'Je porte l'amour de l'antiquité dans mes entrailles,' declared Flaubert in his early years,[1] maintaining in 1852 that he had made all possible efforts to know it and understand it.[2] According to his niece Caroline[3] and his friend Zola,[4] his last plan before his untimely death at the age of fifty-eight was to write his own version of the battle of Thermopylae—unlike his other works, it would at last have been a story about accepted heroes. But the book which best illustrates Flaubert's immensely wide reading of the ancients is *La Tentation de saint Antoine*. In his youth, it had been a *déversoir* for all his longings and interests; in later years, he thoroughly enjoyed revising the episode concerning the death of all the gods. The view of nature taken by the writers of antiquity, for whom nature and God were at first consubstantial, is probably an even more important source of Flaubert's thought than his reading of modern philosophers such as Spinoza, his debt to whom he nevertheless also proclaims with enthusiasm, comparing himself in this with Goethe.[5] 'Retiens donc ceci,' he wrote to Louis Bouilhet in 1850, 'nous sommes trop avancés en fait d'Art pour nous tromper sur la nature.'[6] And, when faced with a series of visions of the interpretations of nature which human beings have devised during the ages, Flaubert's fourth-century hermit Anthony utters a cry of revulsion which we shall show to be of cardinal importance for all Flaubert's works: 'Ignominie! quelle abomination de donner un sexe à Dieu!'[7]

Flaubert was to describe the *mystère, La Tentation de saint Antoine*, as 'l'œuvre de toute ma vie'.[8] Its origins are well known: the annual fairground puppet play with its refrain 'Messieurs les démons, laissez-moi donc!'; Breughel's great canvas, seen at Genoa when he was twenty-three; Callot's engraving, hung above his study fireplace; Creuzer's ten-volume compilation *Les Religions de l'antiquité*.[9] The three versions of *La Tentation* date in turn from 1849, 1856, and 1874. The first diffuse text was never published by Flaubert, but it is

1

enthralling for Flaubert specialists and invaluable for the many insights it provides into his other works. The second reduced version, of which extracts appeared in *L'Artiste*, was welcomed by Baudelaire, who saw in the extracts the 'chambre secrète'[10] of the author's soul and discerned affinities between *mystère* and novel. Finally, the definitive version, much shorter, was still unfinished when its manuscript was buried in the garden at Croisset during the Prussian occupation; having survived the 1870 war it was completed in 1872 and published two years later. Source-book for Symbolism, especially in the visual arts, and again for Surrealism, it was a major influence upon the young Sigmund Freud, who wrote of it as

this book which in the most condensed fashion and with unsurpassable vividness throws at one's head the whole trashy world: for it calls up not only the great problems of knowledge but the real riddles of life, all the conflicts of feelings and impulses; and it confirms the awareness of our perplexity in the mysteriousness that reigns everywhere.

The old gods of India and Egypt, whom Flaubert had studied, the ancient Baals whom he mentions in *Salammbô*, the deities of ancient Italy and of the Northern hemisphere, represented views of the godhead (and thus of nature) as possessing no single sex, but as androgynous, beyond sex, all-productive from their entire being. In other words, they were not anthropomorphic. Nature was a mystery. The scission into sky-god and mother nature, or, more importantly from the point of view of Saint Antoine's protest, the whole conception of nature as mother, will be shown as extremely repugnant to Flaubert.

The notion of an androgynous human being was of interest to the nineteenth century in general. Vigny, Balzac, Gautier, and Stendhal in literature, Gustave Moreau and Odilon Redon in the visual arts, illustrate this preoccupation. The young Flaubert, attracted by what he called a 'hermaphrodite nouveau',[11] saw woman writers in this guise: as he wrote in *Par les champs et par les grèves*, 'chez toutes ces femmes à moitié hommes, la spiritualité ne commence qu'à la hauteur des yeux'.[12] Then later he hoped that the beautiful Louise Colet, poetess and friend of artists, philosophers, politicians and writers, would be for him more than a mistress, a source of 'compagnie dans [son] âme'.[13] Flaubert's master Montaigne, for instance, had written: 's'il se pouvoit dresser une telle accointance, libre et volontaire, où, non seulement les ames eussent cette entiere jouyssance [as in a male friendship] mais encores où les corps [of a man and a woman] eussent part à l'alliance, ou l'homme fust engagé tout entier, il est certain que l'amitié en seroit plus pleine et plus comble.' Montaigne had come to the conclusion that the female sex 'par nul exemple n'y est encore peu arriver',[14] and Flaubert's hopes of his relationship with Louise were also disappointed. From this time onwards, Flaubert's conclusion seems to have been that of Montaigne, whose tastes, opinions, way of life, and *manies* he claimed to share. To Mlle Leroyer de Chantepie he would say that, in view of the difference in their ages, 'nous causons ensemble comme *deux* hommes'.[15] Only in George Sand did he, much later, discern a different type of being, a 'troisième sexe', and with her again his relationship was never sexual. The magnificent correspondence between the two mature writers (1866–76) will contribute importantly to our eventual conclusions.[16]

Blame for the failure of Flaubert's relationship with Louise Colet has in the past been ascribed unequivocally to her. She may indeed have lacked the intelligence and culture to live up to Flaubert's expectations, though it is difficult to believe that some of the things he said to her would be easily accepted by a woman (or a man) of any period. But it is clear that in his eyes she appeared as having let down not only herself but all women. In one of his last letters to her, in April 1854, he wrote:

J'ai toujours essayé (mais il me semble que j'échoue) de faire de toi un hermaphrodite sublime . . . tu m'encombres et me troubles et t'abîmes avec l'élément femelle... Relis même tes œuvres, et tu t'apercevras que tu as en toi un ennemi, un je ne sais quoiqui, en dépit des plus excellentes qualités, du meilleur sentiment et de la plus parfaite conception, t'a rendue ou fait paraître le contraire juste de ce qu'il fallait.[17]

There is undoubtedly, as Jean Bruneau believes,[18] a case for rehabilitating this woman whose acquaintance with Flaubert inspired such superb letters over two periods each lasting three years, letters written from one artist to another with no coquetry and no concessions or condescension, providing an invaluable commentary not only upon the genesis and composition of so original a work as *Madame Bovary*, but upon the activity and nature of the creative consciousness in general. Never again would Flaubert write of his work in such detail; never again, either, would he produce a novel which it is possible to interpret as feminist. Baudelaire, himself author of the remark: 'La femme est naturelle, c'est-à-dire abominable,'[19] said of Flaubert in what remains the best short essay ever written on

Madame Bovary: 'Toutes les femmes *intellectuelles* lui sauront gré d'avoir éleve la femelle à une si haute puissance, si loin de l'animal pur et si près de l'homme idéal.'[20] But after *Madame Bovary,* harking back to more youthful pre-Louise Colet attitudes, Flaubert's pronouncements on women are dominated by indictments. Above all, he condemns what he discerns among his contemporaries, that is, in his own society, as a 'culte de la mère'.[21] Although before he died he seemed in some respects to be changing in his private views, this attitude was enshrined in his works to the very end. Its significance is, I suggest, most evident in the works of imagination, and, Flaubert being of an essentially allegorical and symbolist turn of mind, pursued by 'allégories innombrables' and devoured by 'métaphores incongrues' as he described himself,[22] it can indeed be fully understood only through them. Its corollary is adumbrated in 1876 in Flaubert's appreciation of Renan's tribute to the androgynous muse Athene–Minerva. Speaking on behalf of all his fellow-writers, Renan had implored her: 'Ô noblesse! ô Beauté simple et vraie! déesse dont le culte signifie raison et sagesse, toi dont le temple est une leçon éternelle de conscience et de sincérité ... fais de nous des spiritualistes accomplis ... Le monde ne sera sauvé qu'en revenant à toi, en répudiant ses attaches barbares.'[23] In Flaubert's opinion, all the aspirations of the nineteenth-century intellectual man were there.[24]

Similarly, Alfred de Vigny, though in his masterpiece *La Maison du berger* he was far from repudiating woman as muse (his relations with Louise Colet herself would bring some beauty to his life), left for posthumous publication one of the most devastating of all nineteenth-century condemnations in *La Colère de Samson* and saw the function of the new poetry as an expression of 'l'esprit pur', an aspiration to be carried into practice by Mallarmé. These are tributes of further homage to Athene–Minerva, whose statue we also see in Fantin-Latour's group—now in the Jeu de Paume in Paris—depicting the new visual artists of the day, she whom Plato in the *Timaeus* had long ago designated as the 'souveraine Minerve', 'l'idée élevée à sa plus haute puissance'.

'L'idée' is a term which resounds throughout Flaubert's correspondence, its importance for him being so well-known to his intimates that after his death his niece, in her *Souvenirs intimes,* describes how, following his back-breaking preparation for *Bouvard et Pécuchet* (and much more, though she does not mention them, his financial stresses following her husband's bankruptcy), he had even got to the point of declaring: 'Je me fiche bien de l'Idée!'[25] That Flaubert was profoundly marked by Victor Cousin's translations of Plato is a fact which we find him confirming in so many words to George Sand: 'Je parle en platonicien.'[26] He has just been asserting, as so often throughout his life, that the true aim of art is *la Beauté*, an overriding preoccupation which he found lacking in his 'Naturalist' friends, Daudet and Zola, for instance. He wonders whether a novel cannot produce the same effect as beautiful architecture, as a certain plain but perfect wall on the Acropolis which had made his heart beat faster: 'Dans la précision des assemblages, la rareté des éléments, le poli de la surface, l'harmonie de l'ensemble, n'y a-t-il pas une vertu intrinsèque, une espèce de force divine, quelque chose d'éternel comme un principe?'[27]

The eternal, the unchangeable, the general, as well as the beautiful and the harmonious, are throughout Flaubert's life his reiterated aims. Similarly, where his characters are concerned, the generality of the type was his intention, leading him to reject with some heat suggestions that *Madame Bovary* should be illustrated: 'la plus belle description littéraire est dévorée par le plus piètre dessin . . . Une femme dessinée ressemble à une femme, voilà tout, . . . tandis qu'une femme écrite fait rêver à mille femmes.'[28] In 1870, writing a preface to the posthumously published last poems of his friend Louis Bouilhet, he would particularly appreciate his restriction to the 'côtés immuables de l'âme'.[29] And of Louise Colet's poem *Fantômes* he enquired of her: 'Pourquoi la femme spéciale au lieu de la femme en général?'[30] When writing about a servant girl, bear in mind all women servants, was his injunction. Write with no particular audience in mind, 'sans allusion, sans époque',[31] in the greatest possible human generality. Such determination to 'escape from the mean petty slavery of the particular case' had been described by Plato in the *Symposium*, the dialogue that, along with the *Phaedo*, Flaubert would later recommend to his niece Caroline not only for philosophical study but as magnificent literature.[32]

Platonic, then, is Flaubert's affirmation from an early date of 'l'Idée', its existence, blue and ineffable, a luminous truth, 'seule . . ., éternelle et nécessaire',[33] fit object for the adoration of those who have been called and chosen to create beauty: 'à travers les hideurs de l'existence, contemplons le grand bleu de la poésie, qui est au-dessus et qui reste en place, tandis que tout change et tout passe.'[34] Mallarmé himself would be haunted by no more lofty a notion of art.

Later, in 1857, as he began work on *Salammbô*, Flaubert's aesthetic remains unchanged, his aim being still, so he informs Mlle Leroyer de Chantepie, the woman admirer, much older than he was, whom he was never to meet, 'le Beau indéfinissable résultant de la conception même et qui est la splendeur du Vrai, comme disait Platon'.[35]

Flaubert responded, then, wholeheartedly to the exaltation of what he termed the 'sommets de l'idée',[36] and, in the early great novels particularly, he took literature seriously as concerned with communicating a vision of the truth, 'la conception ... le modèle'.[37] In the novel, it must however be clothed in flesh and blood. 'Ça, c'est de l'Art! Savoir faire l'enveloppe.'[38] The conception nevertheless came first. Flaubert preached to Louise the importance of Goethe's maxim: 'Tout est dans la conception,'[39] and in re-reading the first part of *Madame Bovary* he wished that he could 'd'un seul coup d'œil lire ces cent cinquante-huit pages et les saisir avec tous leurs détails dans une seule pensée'.[40] Later, when preparing *L'Éducation sentimentale,* his initial struggles, so he informed Caroline in 1846, were aimed at the moment when 'l'idée principale s'est dégagée',[41] after which the way ahead was clear.

It is not new to cite Flaubert's own statement that alongside the idealist in him there existed another 'bonhomme' wishing to 'accuser le petit fait' and to make us feel 'presque matériellement' the things he describes,[42] convinced, as he said elsewhere, that no human activity is nobler than 'la contemplation ardente des choses de ce monde',[43] a formula in which the word *ardente* is however the key, combining both Flaubert's activities and suggesting that inner sun of the artist's mind's eye for which he strove: 'Héraclite s'est crevé les yeux pour mieux voir le soleil dont je parle.'[44] To be understood, as would happen to him, entirely on the level of 'le fait historique' and of the observation of social manners was thus a source of great disappointment, not to say irritation, to him. 'Sont-ils bêtes avec leurs observations de mœurs!'[45] he groaned when in 1857 critics of *Madame Bovary* interpreted the novel exclusively in terms of the social preoccupations which had been prescribed for the novel by Balzac. Likewise, his outraged answer years later to adverse criticism of *L'Éducation sentimentale* derives from the same view: when his 'enemy' Barbey d'Aurevilly in *Le Constitutionnel* presented him as the right hand of the Realists and accused him of aiming to 'faire vulgaire', he protested: 'Je me suis toujours efforcé d'aller dans l'âme des choses.'[46]. We should couple this with an assertion he had previously made several times, for instance to Louise during the writing of *Madame Bovary*. 'Laisse donc là ton sexe comme ta patrie, ta religion et ta province. On doit être âme le plus possible et c'est par ce détachement que l'immense sympathie des choses et des êtres nous arrivera plus abondante.'[47]

Not that all critics were mistaken in their reactions. For Baudelaire, Flaubert was, without further comment, 'le poète';[48] for Maupassant, Flaubert's disciple and pupil: 'il suffit de lire avec intelligence *Madame Bovary* pour comprendre que rien n'est plus loin du réalisme.'[49] 'Le réalisme' in contemporary literature, 'ou ce qu'on appelle ainsi', that is, the delineation of facts and concrete details (especially concerning the lower strata of society) for their own sake and as themselves amounting to reality, was, in Flaubert's own words, 'une chose fort laide'.[50] It is therefore highly relevant to our argument here that in 1856 Flaubert should himself have written that it was 'en haine du réalisme'[51] that he had produced *Madame Bovary*; indeed, almost twenty years later, he was still expressing execration of realism to George Sand.[52] Even more important for us is the second part of his original remark: 'Je n'aime pas non plus la fausse idéalité dont nous sommes bernés par le temps qui court.'[53] For, like his admired Cervantes who in *Don Quixote* (to quote Freud's words), 'a great person, himself an idealist, makes fun of his ideals', so Flaubert in *Madame Bovary*, as again in *L'Éducation sentimentale*, showed laughable, regrettable, even blameworthy aspects of the great idealist movement called Romanticism, holding up for questioning, ridicule, or condemnation certain figures—great ones, as well as the second-rate. Nevertheless he would always continue to call himself a 'vieille ganache romantique',[54] a member of 'notre génération, la bonne'. In the same way Baudelaire would always remain for him 'le romantique transcendant que nous aimons'.[55]

'Ah! ce qui manque à la société moderne ... c'est un Aristophane,'[56] he declared during the early stages of composing *Madame Bovary*—'l'immense, le sacro-saint, l'incomparable Aristophane' as he will still be in 1874[57] and who in *The Clouds* had shown a comic version of Plato's own Socrates balanced half-way between heaven and earth, as Emma will visualize the lives of artists and will herself long to be. Moreover, both the 'realism' of the school of literature bearing that name and the false idealism (which Flaubert particularly castigates in the revered figure of Lamartine whose very language consisted of 'phrases femelles'[58]) are, so the texts show, aspects of that same

symbolic 'culte de la mère' which he arraigns in his correspondence.
Both present to the intellect and the sensibility of women as of men a
distorted view of the human position in the face of all nature and
thus, by limiting it in one direction or the other, falsify human life in
all its aspects.

In his works, Flaubert seeks then to see, so far as is possible, with
the eyes of the soul alone, as Plato had prescribed in the *Phaedo:*
'avilis la matière, crache sur ton corps . . . tu te sentiras légère et tout
esprit,' he exclaims in 1853 to Louise.[59] This is the sacrifice required
of the artist, but his gaze must be not only on the horizon but at the
same time on his feet. For in his desire to glimpse luminous truth,
Flaubert rejects those who deny or by their silence imply the denial
of the body. In fact, it is the 'fausse idéalité' that emerges from the
lives of Emma, of Frédéric, and of Salammbô as the major danger.
The *bassesse* of the calculating pursuit of the uniquely material, with
its equally lying denial of 'l'infini dans notre poitrine'—as seen in
Lheureux, Homais, Dambreuse, and all the self-seekers of post-
1848 France, or in Hannon and the Carthaginian protagonists of the
'guerre inexpiable'—await, like nature itself, to engulf and profit from
idealism divorced from experience. Not that the importance of
money as somehow the crutch of the very soul in a modern society is
neglected in Flaubert's world either. Indeed, a major difference
between Emma, who dies along with her illusions, and Frédéric, who
drifts into what Victor Brombert calls 'death-in-life'[60] while salvaging
at least the memory of his dreams, is that Frédéric has a private
income. In other words, as Flaubert said elsewhere, morality has
come to be regarded as a luxury which one can or cannot 'afford'.

More comment on Flaubert's enthusiasm for Aristophanes is
perhaps necessary, for it will be recalled that it was partly on account
of the comic playwright that Plato banished artists from his Republic, objecting to the ridicule he had poured on Socrates the
'meteorologist', that is, upon the latter's wish to relate all human
desires and all material manifestations and occurrences to the
cosmic whole. Flaubert's admiration for Aristophanes is certainly
great. In the rough drafts of *Madame Bovary,* he seems at one point to
be proposing to introduce the baser physical functions into the text
as Aristophanes has them performed on the stage, the presentation
of the whole man being an aspect of Aristophanes' work particularly
applauded by Flaubert.[60] Yet it is Flaubert's echoing of Platonic pre-
scriptions that is the more striking. Not only is there his insistence

that 'l'Idée' (the Forms, as they would be called nowadays) is visible to the soul alone (Flaubert deliberately cultivated nobility of outlook by reading some part of a great classic every day and enjoined Amélie Bosquet never to read mediocre literature[62]), there is also his belief, expressed in 1853, that every soul should be self-sufficient: 'c'est une corruption que de ne pas se suffire à soi-même.'[63] The freedom from envy and hatred to which Flaubert aspired are also required by Plato in the *Timaeus*. Finally, Flaubert's stress on the harmony of the universe and its reproduction in a work of art is Platonic too. 'Habituons-nous à considérer le monde comme une œuvre d'art dont il faut reproduire les procédés dans nos œuvres'[64]: this injunction to Louise in 1853 is a reiteration of a point of view that goes back in Flaubert's life to at least 1846 and was frequently expressed: 'Les plus grands [poètes] ... reproduisent l'Univers, qui se reflète dans leurs œuvres, étincelant, varié, multiple, comme un ciel entier qui se mire dans la mer avec toutes ses étoiles et tout son azur.'[65]

Talk of the soul was very much part of the *Zeitgeist* which formed Flaubert. Apart from the neo-Platonism nourished by the work of Cousin, Victor Hugo, greatest of the French Romantics, had in the *Préface de Cromwell* followed a German conviction—expounded by Goethe among others—whereby Plato's suggestion at the end of the *Symposium* that writers should learn to be comic and tragic at the same time could not come true in literature until the great spiritual experience of the Middle Ages had made it possible. Thus Hugo had seen the distinctive contribution to what he termed 'modern' literature as that of a 'religion spiritualiste'. This religion, so he affirmed, had taught man his double nature: 'qu'il y a en lui un animal et une intelligence, une âme et un corps.'[66] Flaubert's attitude towards Hugo, despite differences of opinion, especially concerning politics and 'démocrasserie', would always remain deeply respectful. In youth, he had been stirred to the depths of his being by the *drames*; under the Second Empire he assisted Louise in sending the exiled 'Crocodile' secret correspondence by way of a London acquaintance; and in maturity when, financially ruined, he heard that he might receive a state pension, he believed it was Hugo, 'un bonhomme simplement exquis',[67] who had been quietly using his influence on his behalf. In 1850, as he settled down to write *Madame Bovary*, it would seem that Flaubert was taking Hugo's manifesto of the Romantic aesthetic seriously as a guide for modern writers. His reading, as reported in his letters to Louise, included most of the works recommended in the *Préface;* the Rouen monster, the *gargouille*, noted by Hugo as typical of the 'modern' imagination,[68] was also, as Flaubert's rough notes show, to have figured originally in the novel[69]—and still discreetly does, as we shall see.

Hugo's affirmation that 'le christianisme sépare profondément le souffle de la matière' and that 'il met un abîme entre l'âme et le corps'[70] was seen by contemporaries, among them the young Flaubert in September 1838,[71] as essential to Hugo's own works, and modern criticism endorses their view that *Notre-Dame de Paris,* for instance, illustrates Hugo's desire to exemplify the dichotomy in a modern art form, in this case the novel, now supplementing the *drame* advocated in the *Préface.* But in Hugo's essay there are simplifications at which Flaubert clearly baulked. Thus, when maintaining that the modern artist must be able to create sublime *types* who will represent the soul 'telle qu'elle est, épurée par la morale chrétienne', Hugo cites young women—Juliet, Desdemona, and Ophelia—as examples of these entirely pure souls. When it comes to the *grotesque,* which must be present also to embody the *bête humaine,* Iago, Tartuffe, Basile, and other villains are enumerated, along with Falstaff, Scapin, and Figaro. All are male.[72]

Now Flaubert, despite bravado and scoffing at eighteen years of age, was no less interested in portraying the dialogue between Hugo's 'animal' and 'intelligence', his *Belle et la Bête,* body and soul, matter and spirit, than the other Romantics among whom he would insistently place himself to the end of his life. His youthful essay on Rabelais, like his piece called *Les Arts et le commerce* (1839), already rails at a modern Europe which goes far towards remedying physical deprivations while denying the 'gouffre béant' in the breast of all men,[13] and although, as we have seen, his social thinking matured into a less trenchant estimate of this problem, the greatest facing a materialistic, machine-dominated society, it is possible to say that the bulk of his works are illustrations of his basic preoccupation. The early 'metaphysical journeys' are explicitly adventures of the soul. Then there is the Faust-like Saint Antoine; Emma Bovary who, in Baudelaire's words, was equally tempted by 'tous les démons de l'illusion . . . toutes les lubricités de la matière environnante';[74] Salammbô, seemingly unattainable, in turn attracted and repelled by Mâtho, 'la bête fauve', and finally expiring along with him. *L'Éducation sentimentale* is a treatment of the theme in a wide and deeply significant sense; likewise the *Trois Contes,* where we have the struggle within Julien between a desire for innocence and an instinct to murderous violence, and that within Antipas between the forces incarnate in the solar Iaokanann—'malgré moi je l'aime'[75]—and those represented by his wife Hérodias, with whom his links are largely physical and who—Cybele flanked with lions—is evoked in terms of the very earth.

And yet Flaubert does not subscribe to clear-cut divisions, as all the texts also show. It is well known that for this son of a Voltairean surgeon, brought up in the hospital itself and accustomed to the sight of fly-infested cadavers, the flesh, its corruption and its passing, loomed large in his conception of the human being and thus of nature. The sight of a beautiful woman on the dissecting table, he wrote in 1837, with her guts stretched above her head, changes our notion of her.[76] Then, during 1846, Flaubert had also studied the lives of certain saints, 'pas du tout dans l'intention de me donner la Foi, mais pour voir les gens qui ont la Foi',[77] and in them he had been able to register the hair-fine distinction separating physical and spiritual longings and frustrations. This borderline between soul and body, its whereabouts so difficult to establish, was the area that interested him, as it would Freud. He felt strongly that neither doctors nor philosophers had so far sufficiently studied human nature from this point of view. During his own mental illness neither had been of much avail, and it was to his own efforts that he owed his eventual recovery: 'Les matérialistes et les spiritualistes empêchent également de connaître la matière et l'esprit parce qu'ils scindent l'un de l'autre.'[78] Thus in 1846 Flaubert told Louise that two years spent on metaphysics had been so much wasted time.[79] Nevertheless his life will show that his intention would always be to devote his unremitting efforts to serving an artistic tradition which had introduced into human life a 'je ne sais quoi d'aérien', something 'au-dessus d'elle-même', as plainly stated in his preface to Louis Bouilhet's *Dernières Chansons* in 1872.[80]

Thus, when starting on *Madame Bovary,* Flaubert needed to reconcile three motive forces: first, his Platonic idealism; secondly, his wish to debunk, as Aristophanes had, the exaggerated idealism of his contemporaries (the danger of which he was aware of in his own nature); and thirdly, his desire to learn from and put into practice (or reject as the case might be) Hugo's formula for a tragic-comic, sublime and grotesque, 'modern' work of art.

As he began, he described himself fittingly as having 'le regard penché sur les mousses de moisissure de l'âme'.[81] At the same time he knew that 'ce mot d'âme a fait dire presque autant de bêtises qu'il y a d'âmes'.[82] In particular, he disapproved of false spirituality in all the arts, the fact that, if a sculptor produced a statue of a woman visibly capable of breast-feeding, for instance, he would be accused of sensuality, whereas a less evidently female figure would find favour for a spurious 'idealism' and 'spirituality'.[83] Then the opulent painters of the Venetian school who were his favourites were held by others (Maxime du Camp for example) to be materialists, while for him they were great colourists and 'de crânes poètes'.[84] In literature also, he declared, 'la couleur' was too materialistic in the eyes of 'le bon sens français' astride its peaceful nag, scared of being swept to the skies by too many metaphors.[85] Much worse and infinitely dangerous to women while encouraging hypocrisy in men was, for Flaubert, the 'amour éthéré'[86] which figures in the work of Lamartine, whom he considered both a poor poet and a poor politician, characteristics which *L'Éducation sentimentale* shows not to be unconnected. What is more, women took this version of love and the female seriously. They were told by men that they were angels, and 'de pauvres anges' was what they believed themselves to be. All the 'embêtements bleuâtres du lyrisme poitrinaire'[87] of Lamartine's works are to blame for much that is wrong in modern France; he even goes so far as to say that they are responsible for the arrival of the Second Empire. And in Flaubert's texts, Lamartine's poem *Le Lac*, which the tragic Emma, 'une femme de fausse poésie et de faux sentiments',[88] sings to Léon as they are rowed back to Rouen from their idyllic island, calling upon time to stand still ('Ô temps, suspends ton vol!'), emerges as falsity, hubris, irony, in the context of Part III of *Madame Bovary*, in which clocks, bells, rowlocks that sound like a metronome, all stress its ineluctable passage. Likewise the notion that all nature will retain a trace of the poet's love for Elvire: 'Que ... Tout dise: ils ont aimé.' For, as Charles looks up at the vine in his misery and anger after Emma's death, 'pas une feuille n'en bougea'. And when her father had ridden through the countryside, wondering at the sense of Homais's complicated letter, he had been unable to believe that she was dead, for nothing in nature had changed. 'Tout, dans mon œuvre, doit l'irriter!'[89] was Flaubert's astonished reaction when Lamartine defended *Madame Bovary* at the time of its trial for corruption of religion and morals, and in fact upon closer inspection Lamartine's enthusiasm would wane. Flaubert's objections to Lamartine's Italian idyll *Graziella* in 1852 had been violent. 'La baise-t-il ou ne la baise-t-il pas?!'[90] Does he sleep with her or doesn't he? To etherealize biology in this way is for Flaubert 'sale'.[91] It is not only to tell a woman a lie but also to render unto biology the ultimate homage. This, to Flaubert, is anathema. Again it is useful to turn to Plato, this time as explained by Plutarch whose *Moralia* Flaubert studied at length while writing *Madame Bovary.* There we read: 'Plato is wont to give to the conceptual the name of idea, example or father, and to the material the name of mother.' Remembering then that Flaubert is essentially of an allegorical and symbolist turn of mind in his great effort to attain to 'l'Idée', we shall come to understand Flaubert's objections to 'le culte de la mère'. By it he also means at a second symbolic level—in the context of an acclamation (naïve or self-interested) of a largely spurious idealism and a false spirituality engendering hypocrisy—the worship of matter.

Linked with this is the stress placed in the literature admired by his contemporaries upon sexual love, presented as though it were the only form of love and the sole source of self-fulfilment for women and of redemption for men, making of it, as Flaubert complained to and about Louise, 'un tambour pour régler le pas de l'existence'. When Bouvard and Pécuchet came to read *Adolphe, La Nouvelle Héloïse,* and the novels of Mme de Staël, they would lament as Flaubert had: 'Le cœur seul est traité, toujours du sentiment! Comme si le monde ne contenait pas autre chose!'[92] In Flaubert's work, as we shall see, it is the saving Eros of the end of the *Symposium,* life-force and fount of all forms of joy and creativity, which emerges as fit study and valid aspiration. His portrayal of love as bringing in its wake disillusion, irony, tragedy, intensifies the strength of his profound and comprehensive vision. Always, even in the so-called 'oriental' works, although rarely formulated until *Bouvard et Pécuchet,* there is present a deep concern for his own epoch whose progressive politics, neo-catholicism, and allegedly anti-traditional art he mostly deplored, while maintaining that even so he was a revolutionary to the marrow of his bones.[93] Similarly, for all his inveighing against women, culminating in his plans for a novel in a Second-Empire setting whose theme was to be 'la dégradation de l'Homme par la Femme',[94] he nevertheless wrote in one of his notebooks: 'celui qui ne dit pas de mal des femmes ne les aime point, puisque la manière la plus profonde de sentir quelque chose est d'en souffrir.'[95]

It is time now to turn to the elements in Flaubert's life which, alongside his reactions to the artistic scene of the epoch, determined the powerful originality of his first masterpiece, *Madame Bovary.*

CHAPTER TWO

'Madame Bovary, c'est moi'

Les bourgeois ne se doutent guère que nous leur servons notre
cœur.[1]

'Madame Bovary, c'est moi, d'après moi' is probably Gustave
Flaubert's most celebrated remark, allegedly made to his friend,
Amélie Bosquet, novelist and historian of Norman folklore. The
words ring true but surprise us coming from this apostle of detach-
ment from the ephemeral and the accidental, for whom above all
'c'est là ce qu'il y a de moins fort au monde, parler de soi'.[2]

This remark has been much discussed, but the sense in which
Flaubert means it may be illuminated by a comment made by
François Mauriac who, while objecting to the biographical approach
to literature and envying Shakespeare the obscurity which
surrounds most of his life, has this to say: 'Un écrivain ne se confie ni
à sa Correspondance ni même à ses journaux intimes. Seules ses
créatures racontent sa véritable histoire.' It is a secret history, which a
certain *pudeur* prevents him from enunciating openly, which he does
not himself know entirely, until it can eventually find expression and
arrive at its conclusion, indeed even exorcise itself, by means of
representative personages and situations. The Gustave Flaubert
who, at the age of roughly thirty, sat down to write *Madame Bovary*,
had known a severe mental illness at the age of twenty-three,
followed by the deaths in quick succession of his distinguished
surgeon father, still at the height of his powers, of his only sister
Caroline, to whom he had been very close, and finally, only two years
later, of his beloved friend Alfred Le Poittevin. Pain and mortality, a
'plaie profonde toujours cachée',[3] are at the heart of this tragic story,
which is yet for some a comic masterpiece, set in a milieu which
Flaubert chose deliberately, reflecting his overall view of modern life
as well as of art.

Rarely does Flaubert speak of his sister's death in his letters. Only
to his mother, writing during his journey through the East, does he

15

say: 'Le souvenir de mon pauvre rat ne me quitte pas. J'ai toujours à
son endroit une place vide au cœur et que rien ne comble.'[4] And
arriving at Cana, he cannot bear to go into the church[5] because of his
memories of Veronese's picture in the Louvre showing Christ's first
miracle, the turning at a wedding feast of water into wine, colour of
the blood Christ eventually spilt on the Cross, of the blood vomited
by Caroline, so recently a bride, and later by Emma, poisoned by her
own hand but also as an outcome of a series of events which had
begun with her marriage, and even earlier by the fact of her ever
meeting Charles, an event which moreover took place on the very
day of the wedding at Cana—6 January. The recurrence of the colour
of blood is a basic image in the novel, as we shall see in more detail.
Nor does the parallel shock, for the passion of the Son of Man pre-
figures the destiny of all men, and of women too. 'Tirelessly the Fates
repeat a thousand times the old story of the falling night,' wrote
Goethe to Zelter on the death of the latter's son. For Flaubert, the
task of the writer, male or female, is to take upon himself all the
passions of the world.[6]

A lofty notion of the mission of the poet is fundamental to the
Romantic ethos, and in nineteenth-century literature alongside
Christ Himself, 'l'éternelle victime', brother of Icarus and of Attys,
who is overtly claimed by Gérard de Nerval as a prefiguration of the
artist,[7] there walks another proto-Christ, Orpheus, delightful *pâtre*
and singer upon the lyre. Professor Riffaterre has noted that,
although never actually mentioned by Flaubert's close friend
Bouilhet, Orpheus is discernible in his works.[8] It was impossible for
Flaubert not to know the poetic scene of his time, given his relations
with Bouilhet and with Louise, and it is the contemporary epic poem
which is of particular interest here. Flaubert's first version of his
mystère Saint Antoine had been modelled on Quinet's prose poem
Ahasvérus, and it was Flaubert's belief, stated in the correspondence,
that the latest development in literature, 's'éthérisant' as he thought it
had been through the ages (that is, appealing progressively less to the
senses, expressing—as we have already seen Flaubert's aim to be—
the psyche in so far as possible), was the replacement of the epic in
verse by the novel in prose.[9] Alfred de Vigny had said as much in his
time, but, after attempts such as *Stello* and with an unfinished
Daphné still on his hands, he had returned to verse in *Les Destinées*.
For Flaubert, the very style of the new novel was to be that of the
epic.[10]

Now a favourite theme in the statuary of Flaubert's period was the group Psyche and Eros. Pradier, in whose studio Flaubert had met Louise Colet, sculpted more than one Psyche, while the young Flaubert had himself been delighted with a *Psyche and Eros* by the eighteenth-century artist Canova, which he had seen in the Villa Carlotti[11] and of which an example is now in the permanent collection at the Louvre. In the scenarios of *Madame Bovary*, an unspecified 'Canova' was to have figured in the salon at Yonville.[12] It is perhaps not too fanciful to suggest that Flaubert had the Psyche and Eros group in mind and that he repressed the statue as at the same time unrealistic in such a background and also as being too obvious a hint to us. For that matter, Canova and his pupils sculpted many a Psyche, and the presence of one of his pieces in Flaubert's original conception of *Madame Bovary* cannot but be encouraging to my point of view. Perhaps, similarly, the Pradier which (this time realistically) would stand upon the mantleshelf in Jacques Arnoux's office in *L'Éducation sentimentale* had a kindred subject? Certainly it was one which we know to have continued to charm Flaubert, for the 1931 catalogue for the Franklin-Grout sale contained a bronze mantleshelf set by Clésinger—a clock and two candelabras—which also figures Psyche and Eros and which was Flaubert's wedding present to his niece Caroline. An example of the set (Clésinger made two) can be seen at the Musée Marmottan in Paris. Subjects from the story of Psyche are also treated in paintings of the period by Gérard, Picot, and Pierre-Paul Prud'hon that are now in the Louvre. As for the literature of the period, the poet Laprade had written an epic poem *Psyché* in 1841. Moreover, the subtitle of Lamartine's epic *Jocelyn* had been *Psyché*. Given Flaubert's attitude towards Lamartine and his 'school', together with Lamartine's declared aim in *La Chute d'un ange* to describe 'la métempsycose d'une âme dégradée', we may see that Flaubert is indeed taking up a common preoccupation of his contemporaries and vying with their treatment of it. For 'la métempsycose d'une âme dégradée' describes Emma. She is, in Flaubert's own words at the time of the book's trial, 'un caractère de femme naturellement corrompu'.[13] Her lot in life denies her transcendence, notably in the 'forme convenue' which she had been conditioned to require by her reading, by the particular type of semi-mystical religiosity imparted to her at the convent, and by the general attitude towards the young ladies with whom she identifies herself after her schooling. The progress of Emma from unusual

candeur (a key word in Flaubert's presentation of her) to what most
will see as final degradation can be seen as a deliberate attempt to
rival Lamartine's intention, but in prose, muscular, rhythmic, packed
with content, multiple, varied, infinitely suggestive—and epic.

It is my contention, then, that the story of Psyche and Eros
underpins *Madame Bovary*. Personal names can be symbolic in
Flaubert's works, and indeed can form part of the patterns of
imagery; they are, in Flaubert's own words, 'une chose capitale',[14] and
once incorporated into a work after much groping, they are
completely unchangeable, as in an allegory. Now *Ema*, anagram of
âme, was the name of the heroine in an eighteenth-century allegory
dealing with the relationship between the soul and the senses,[15] and,
although there is no proof that Flaubert read the book, the idea is
shown, by its existence, to be feasible. Thus it is my belief that
Flaubert has advisedly adopted the name Emma (a particularly
Norman name, what is more) for this, his first relation of the Psyche
myth.

A further point of interest with regard to representations of the
human soul comes in a book written by Alfred Maury, Flaubert's
revered friend. The book in question, *Essai sur les légendes pieuses
du Moyen Age* (1843), has been proved to be an early source of *Saint
Julien l'Hospitalier*, first meditated upon by Flaubert when *Madame
Bovary* was still in progress.[16] In it, Maury shows how the earliest
representation of the human soul in remote art was an 'androgyne',
indicating a primitive view of the soul, the breath of life, before the
encroachment of the artificial over-differentiation of the sexes that
Flaubert summed up in these words: '*La femme est un produit de
l'homme. Dieu a créé la femelle et l'homme a fait la femme*; elle est le
résultat de la civilisation, une œuvre factice.'[17]

What is our first view of Emma? 'Ce qu'elle avait de beau, c'étaient
les yeux.' Her lips, however, are sensual, and we see her biting them.
We are back with the faces of the intellectual women noted in *Par les
champs et par les grèves*, of whom, as was pointed out earlier,
Flaubert wrote that their spirituality only began at the eyes: 'tout le
reste est resté dans les instincts matériels.'[18] Baudelaire's words about
'une âme virile dans un charmant corps feminin' likewise stress the
androgynous nature of the human spirit whose history we are to
read, emphasizing indeed her early aspiration to be spirit first and
foremost, by comparing her to 'Pallas, surgie tout armée de la tête de
son père'.[19] We have already had occasion to notice Athene–Minerva

as representing, traditionally as she always has, pure spirit and pure intelligence — striven for by certain of Flaubert's contemporary artists. Now Athene–Minerva is alone among classical goddesses in being mentioned in the text of *Madame Bovary*, where, on our first acquaintance with Emma, we find her portrait, drawn by Emma's hand when at school, framed in gold and pinned upon the kitchen wall. It was originally to have had a cracked glass, but Flaubert suppressed so obvious and premature an indication of decadence from an ideal.[20] For Emma too will attempt to emulate the bold-eyed goddess who, as Flaubert inserted into Louise Colet's poem *L'Acropole d'Athènes*, was the original 'mère d'Athènes', city of pure form and of aspiration to pure beauty, to be replaced, alas, as time wore on by 'Vénus impudique', or so Flaubert wished Louise to recount in her poem.[21] The parallel will prove interesting.

Here then is Flaubert's heroine: Psyche, called Emma and evoking the androgyne, Pallas Athene, a lorgnette tucked into her corsage to stress the point. Flaubert, using one of his poetic devices, has superimposed various images one upon the other in this first view of Emma, each leading into the development of certain facets of her character: nineteenth-century intellectual woman (however inadequate her training and ability, the urge to learn is there), possessed of unusual *candeur*, that is, innocence and a basic naïveté, recalling Apuleius' description of the 'simple-hearted' Psyche. Finally Emma has pretensions and a weakness for the trappings of appearance, most important in the evolution of the psyche as seen by writers in the later ancient world. Apuleius' superlative narration of the tale of *Psyche and Eros* is the most important example. Flaubert would have read in Creuzer that for the allegorical minds of the ancients the fall of the soul in this tale away from its pristine purity is essentially an ever greater engagement in the toils of appearance, that is, of matter, the temptations of the matter which surrounds us, as Baudelaire described them.

When Flaubert mentions the 'tête de Minerve' on the kitchen wall at Les Bertaux, he notes that the inscription upon it has been written by Emma in 'lettres gothiques'. Now the medieval and later version of Psyche and Eros is, of course, *La Belle et la Bête*, though Perrault was hard put to it to understand the equivalence he knew to exist between them in the preface to his seventeenth-century edition.[22] Flaubert's handbook to the study of the past, Creuzer's vast examination of ancient religions with special reference to their symbolisms, has no such difficulty. Psyche and Eros, he states with simplicity, represent the soul and the body, just as Hugo interpreted *La Belle et la Bête* in the *Préface de Cromwell*.

Before looking further into this antithesis and its representation in *Madame Bovary*, let us deepen our study of the early Emma. The Gothic lettering of her interpretation we shall learn to see as an indication that, if our first sight of her with her *candeur* and her bold stare calls to mind Homer and the early Greek representation of pure spirit whose portrait hangs on her wall, by the end of the book our vision of her will have been brought up to date in the 'vieille cité normande' of Rouen with its Gothic cathedral and Gothic quarter (in Flaubert's early versions Rouen was to be described as 'la cité gothique'[23]). The colour of her eyes, for instance, will no longer be dark nearing to black. They will be blue, for she has evolved, as the book proceeds, into a Northern heroine. But was the colour of Athene–Minerva's eyes black? Hers were surely green. Was it not Venus, the blackness of whose eyes had been stressed by Homer?

Here is the parable within the parable. For when Aphrodite–Venus took upon herself to try to spin Athene's web, did the thread not break in her hands? The significance of this, so Flaubert could have read in Benjamin Constant's book on the history of religions[24] as well as in Creuzer, is the treachery and inadequacy of matter. And is not this the story of Emma? *Madame Bovary* is, at the most conceptual level, an allegory of the changes which come over the human psyche between birth and death, of a sensual being striving unsuccessfully and eventually perversely to be pure spirit, to be intellect and aspiration, as well as the 'instincts matériels' which the young Flaubert had so automatically identified as female. Through all the actions—selfish, dishonest, and plain silly—which we may find it difficult to accept in her, Emma is still, in Baudelaire's words, seeking that elusive goal so stressed in the early nineteenth century, 'l'Idéal'.[25] When writing *Madame Bovary*, Flaubert commented upon how aspirations of a noble nature—'des élans d'idéalisme . . . l'aspiration éthérée de la souveraine joie'—aimed, as in Emma's case, at deliverance from both the 'dépendances de la loi' and the 'mollesses de la chair', can become degraded to the level of 'les appétits matériels les plus furieux', 'les extravagances charnelles les plus immondes'.[26] While not exaggerating the extent of the downfall of Emma—for, thief, adulteress, and bad mother though she is, she would seem to many readers (Sartre, one presumes) no more guilty as an individual than would Faust—we appreciate the value of Flaubert's remarks on the perversion of appetite and will see their relevance for all his women characters, right through to the symbolic dance of Salome, which also begins as that of a 'Psyché curieuse'.[27] To them we may add his further words concerning the savage reactions of the unsatisfied human spirit: 'Notre âme est une bête féroce; toujours affamée, il faut la gorger jusqu'à la gueule pour qu'elle ne se jette pas sur nous.' As so often when we read Flaubert, modern society in general, as well as the history of Emma and of the past, is here tragically called to mind.

So far, then, we have seen superimposed within Emma: Psyche, Pallas Athene, and, finally, Venus striving to emulate her illustrious artist sibling. Emma, who tries to spin the web of her own life (for the importance of spinning and weaving in *Madame Bovary*, see below, Chapter Five) fails comparably. How, asks Flaubert in one of his notebooks, does it come about that the noble goddess Venus Urania (*alter ego* of Athene) descended through the ages to a depraved level, Venus 'amour de la forme' becoming a 'putain'?[28] In the episode of the gods in *Saint Antoine*, Flaubert's Venus again retraces her own career in much the same terms. And this too, as we shall show, is the story of Emma, who, alas, declines from unusual *candeur* (such, for instance, as no other of Rodolphe's mistresses had ever possessed) to a state of mind where she is ready to sell herself 'sans se douter le moins du monde de sa prostitution'. Her failure to *recognize* what she has become is particularly noteworthy, as this is for Flaubert a feature of his whole age, as is made clear in *L'Éducation sentimentale*. Louise Colet's high-minded strictures about 'les filles', while at the same time depending on her lovers for assistance of all kinds, including money, cannot be irrelevant to this conclusion of the career of Emma–Venus.

To return to the anagram *Emma/Âme*, it is extremely interesting to note that Guignault's translation of Creuzer quotes certain nineteenth-century scholars as positing that a similar inversion of the name of the Egyptian goddess of the spirit, Neith, was the origin of the name Athene, an equivalence already suggested by Plato. For an analogical mind such as Flaubert's, this knowledge must have provided encouragement. But this would not necessarily be of any importance if it were not for the great vogue for everything Egyptian, as well as 'Orphic' (indeed, Creuzer points out that for Herodotus 'Orphic' and 'Egyptian' were synonymous) which characterized nineteenth-century France—'la rage permanente de l'Egypte', to quote Flaubert's words in *Par les champs et par les grèves*.[29] Flaubert, with his interest in ancient religions and civilizations, travelled to Egypt, as we have seen, like many other writers including Lamartine and Nerval. Now Emma is an inhabitant of Normandy, and among the great enthusiasts for Egypt and things Egyptian was the school of Norman and Breton Celticists for which Flaubert did not conceal his scorn. In *Par les champs*, after studying the question with what he assures Louise Colet is scholarly thoroughness,[30] he concludes that the Celtic contribution to historical monuments consisted entirely of 'des pierres'[31]—unidentifiable stones of a primitive character—and that all the explanations put forward concerning their function and origin are so much nonsense. Flaubert is extremely witty about those of his contemporaries who took so seriously the putative glories of their forebears. When Bouvard and Pécuchet come to study the subject, the humour is even more scathing. What is the relevance here?

The great word which had linked both cultures in the minds of the Celticists was the place-name Sais. Now it is from Sais in Egypt that Neith travelled to Athens and became Athene, so Creuzer has it. Similarly, it is the name Saez (or Sées) in the Orne that leads the amateur Celticists whom Flaubert found so comic to see the origins of their own civilization in Egypt. Flaubert will himself travel to Saez when preparing *Bouvard et Pécuchet*.

The Egyptian Sais was, precisely, the cult-centre of Neith–Athene. What is more, another name now enters our view of this composite goddess whose development is contained within Emma. This is Isis, whose name, so we learn from Plutarch, was openly connected, again at Sais, with Athene. Plutarch alone in the ancient world systematized the religion of Isis and Osiris—in the *Moralia* which, as we have seen, Flaubert read over a long period while composing *Madame Bovary*. Plutarch tells us that at Sais there was a statue of Athene, 'whom they believe to be Isis'. Likewise, 'they oftentimes call Isis by the name of Athene'. The name Isis, so we are further informed by Plutarch, was said, like the name Athene, to mean a 'lover of wisdom'. Moreover, she is connected by Plato—for here again is this cardinal force in Flaubert's life and work—with 'essence' and 'sense', and thus often called Athene.

Like Athene (indeed, another name for her) and like Venus Urania (that is, the goddess in her stellar and non-material aspect), there is then another goddess who, in the early stages of human attempts to conceptualize Nature, stood for wisdom, essence, sense. Summing up all the goddesses (that is, visions of nature) is one further attribute with which the ancients endowed Isis, namely, that she was 'many-eyed'. Has not Flaubert superimposed upon his evocations of these androgynous goddesses aiming to attain to pure reason, their flashing eyes developing through the book from dark brown, black to blue, the ever-evolving figure of Isis, both anterior and posterior to all the others, as Nerval describes her in a near-contemporaneous text?[32]

What justification would Flaubert have for this vision, in a modern Psyche, of a composite goddess? His reading list, as indicated in his letters to Louise Colet, again lends support to our interpretation, even though a knowledge of contemporary references to Isis might in any case have made all clear to us. Does Flaubert mention Isis? Indeed he does: in 1853 he calls upon Louise Colet with great enthusiasm to read in Apuleius' *Golden Ass* Lucius' invocation to the goddess Isis and her reply to him.[33] The answer and illumination to Lucius are that Isis is in fact all the great goddesses. Many are their names, but one is their identity, the lady Isis herself:

> You can see me here, Lucius, in answer to your prayer. I am Nature, the universal Mother, mistress of all the elements, primordial child of time, sovereign of all things spiritual, queen of the dead, queen also of the immortals, the single manifestation of all gods and goddesses that are. My nod governs the shining heights of Heaven, the wholesome sea-breezes, the lamentable silences of the world below.

She is, then, queen of Heaven, earth, sea, and the underworld, and we cannot but think of Charles's view of the Emma he worshipped: 'L'univers entier n'excédait pas le tour soyeux de son jupon.'

An interesting point will very likely have struck the reader by now. Both this cardinal text, identifying all the goddesses as nature, and the beautiful telling of the tale of Psyche and Eros appear in a single book—Apuleius' *Golden Ass*. By this late period in Rome, then, heir to so much that was Greek and Egyptian, the androgynous human soul of earliest art and the androgynous prefigurations of nature have both become female as they were in the Syrian and Near Eastern religions. They are Psyche and the great goddess, who, as we have seen, contains within herself not only all the goddesses but also all the gods. All nature has thus become anthropomorphized as a female and in particular as the Mother. If woman, as Flaubert had upheld in a letter to Louise Colet, is 'une œuvre factice',[34] so, logically, the soul as female *anima* and nature as female, the Universal Mother, are equally factitious, equally artificial, the products of civilization.

A symbolic 'culte de la mère' has thus been extended beyond woman to the human spirit itself and to nature, all of which are seen in terms one of another. Comparisons with Romanticism and the nineteenth century in general readily come to mind, as we shall see. But, before considering Flaubert's relationship with his contemporaries and with the whole tradition of the treatment in modern literature of the feminine, it is interesting to recall a few well-known facts concerning Flaubert's own conditioning and aspirations in the generation to which Emma belonged and which came in so many ways to an end with the December *coup d'état* in 1851, a theme which is made clearer in *L'Éducation sentimentale.* Emma's ardent temperament, given to revery, was Flaubert's own. His instincts for luxury in modest financial circumstances, even absurd dreams of *bayadères* upon oriental divans, contributed to his picture of Emma. He would not attempt to deny that in his own youth he had been 'parfaitement ridicule',[35] for self-criticism is a part of self-depiction. His analysis of Emma was, he averred, based upon himself.[36] In writing, he whipped himself until he drew blood, figuratively speaking. His own high dreams, his own former agonizing boredom as a student of the law, a subject alien to him and to all his dearest interests, help to explain why Emma's collapse rings so true.

A human psyche that has learned to aspire spiritually and sensually, however inadequately, will, when deprived, flutter and die or else become dègraded, as Flaubert shows in Emma and as Creuzer comments in his analysis of the Psyche story. One solution exists—that open to Flaubert himself. For, though understanding all the yearnings for a different sort of society which beset Emma, and though sharing in the pursuit of the ideal which Baudelaire discerned in her, though participating, indeed, to an even higher degree in a distaste for the onerous, purely physical side of being alive, Flaubert, conquered or, as he himself might have said, 'elevated' the Emma within him. He too knew what it was to wish to escape into 'les espaces immaculés'. But unlike her, whose temperament was, we are specifically told, 'plus sentimentale qu'artiste' and who passes from panacea to panacea, each tossed aside in a manner Flaubert noted elsewhere as characteristic of his whole generation (Du Camp,

Louise Colet, and later his own creation Frédéric), Flaubert discovered his task in this life and persevered along a 'ligne droite'. Flaubert's view of mankind resembling Plato's in the *Republic*, he could declare that an ideal world would be one in which each individual, having found his personal bent, lived in accordance with it. Now for Flaubert, being born an artist meant that he studied the world and nature for their own sake and not for his own. In this he differs from Louise Colet and from so many Romantic writers who follow in the steps of Jean-Jacques Rousseau. The view of nature he applauded in the works of Apuleius is one which presents 'la Nature pour elle-même'.[37] And if Flaubert chooses his representative woman in the mediocre surroundings he was to make his special field, he made the choice even *because* it was so repugnant to him, in search of that very probability which seemed to him more scientific, and knowing that the mediocre is, above all, the realm of that tragic state, illusion.

What of other examples of the treatment of the eternal feminine? Thus, for instance, at the first sight of Beatrice, Dante, known to Flaubert since his early teens, felt most beautifully the pricking of the growth of the wings of love. The neo-Platonists of the sixteenth century (which, in a *Carnet*, Flaubert referred to as carrying on 'la tradition' more authentically than the 'grand siècle') believed that woman might afford some glimpse of the ideal form of beauty. Much more recently, in *La Nouvelle Héloïse*, Rousseau, whose 'petit-fils' Flaubert owned that he was,[38] had invented a memorable mother-figure in Julie. At the end of Part Two of *Faust*, that 'maître homme' Goethe had shown Gretchen beckoning the hero onwards and upwards to salvation: 'Das Ewig-Weibliche zieht uns hinan.' Men are redeemed, also, by woman in the French poetry of the time as well as in Rousseau—Laprade, Ballanche, l'abbé Constant, Quinet, like Balzac and Lamartine, subscribed to the idealized notion of a 'femme-ange', embodiment for Flaubert of the false spirituality noted in the previous chapter. All three of the men in Emma's life address her in these terms. But in Flaubert's novel the word is also there so that he can deny the very notion; it is easier, so he argues, to portray an angel than a woman, because the wings dissimulate the hump.[39] Not for Flaubert, as Goethe had confessed of himself to Eckermann, fictional women who were better than those he had met in reality. Flaubert abandoned his first idea of depicting a provincial modern mystic (though with no mission for redemption that he ever mentioned) precisely because Emma, upon whom his choice finally settled, seemed to him a woman such as one meets in actual life.[40]

In contrast to woman as redemptress and as guiding hand in transcendence upwards towards the divine and the beautiful, Emma is more like a female Don Juan, taking the character in its most interesting non-cliché form, as Flaubert had begun to do in extracts from an abandoned project later published by Maupassant.[41] The Don, another soul in search of purity, seeks it perversely and exclusively in sexual adventures, which swamp and divert some of his magnificent rebelliousness and passion for liberty. Emma, like him, is caused by Flaubert to descend, apparently damned, into the abyss, fetched and guided as he was, in her case by the blind man—'dans les ténèbres éternelles, comme un épouvantement'. Once dead, Emma, again in contrast to Gretchen, will seem to be dragging Charles down towards her. 'Elle le corrompait par-delà le tombeau.' The chaste Diana the huntress, parodied as Emma in riding-habit ('en amazone') and whom Rodolphe did not seduce without some trouble, has become Diana the infernal, that is, Hecate herself, whose dogs howl in the distance after Emma's death, for there is yet more prey left in the Bovary family.

As for Flaubert's contemporaries, his view is this: 'Il n'est pas un écrivain qui n'ait exalté la mère, l'épouse ou l'amante ... la génération endolorie larmoie sur les genoux des femmes, comme un enfant malade. On n'a pas l'idée de la lâcheté des hommes envers elles.'[42] We recognize a further reference to 'le culte de la mère', here clearly identified with submission to all females—'sur les genoux des femmes'—and ascribed to Flaubert's whole generation. Elsewhere he will go further, speaking of 'ce pauvre siècle à scrofules et à pâmoisons ... qui se complaît sur les genoux féminins, comme un enfant malade'.[43] A tendency of his whole epoch is in question, and, with his affair with Louise Colet at an end and *Madame Bovary,* that investigation of a female psyche, also complete, he will round upon all women as a sex. Other sallies are well known: 'Je crois ... qu'une des causes de la faiblesse morale du dix-neuvième siècle vient de sa poétisation exagérée.'[44] Yet all three of these attacks upon the female species were in fact written in letters to individual women. Flaubert's hostility is towards some element which he called symbolically rather than literally 'la femme', the enemy within herself, as he had told Louise, 'l'élément féminin',[45] which is, as he also said, the work of the male. Flaubert's studies of Salammbô, supplemented by his portraits in *L'Éducation sentimentale,* will contribute to a full understanding of his meaning, culminating in that allegory of the Second Empire which is *Hérodias,* where the dance of Salome expresses in terrifying fashion the power of the eternal feminine.[46]

The equivalence between Emma and an over-poeticized figure of the eternal feminine is made clear in a number of ways, notably in Léon's famous composite portrait:

Par la diversité de son humeur, tour à tour mystique ou joyeuse, babillarde, taciturne, emportée, nonchalante, elle allait rappelant en lui mille désirs, évoquant des instincts ou des réminiscences. Elle était l'amoureuse de tous les romans, l'héroïne de tous les drames, le vague *elle* de tous les volumes de vers. Il retrouvait sur ses épaules la couleur ambrée de l'odalisque au bain; elle avait le corsage long des châtelaines féodales; elle ressemblait aussi à *la femme pâle de Barcelone,* mais elle était par-dessus tout Ange!

All these elements—Egyptian, medieval, Romantic Spanish, Romantic French—are the invention of males—writers, painters, musicians. And although aiding and abetting as women will in the confection of this vaporous persona, Emma is its victim and will be abandoned when the time comes for 'settling down'. Neither worship of the 'ange-femme' nor 'le culte de la mère' imply feminism. Both are accompanied by a 'souverain mépris', as Flaubert himself once said,[47] for actual, individual women. The relationship is false, an aspect of the *Blague* that Flaubert so detested. The very idealization of a fictitious feminine is a lie, as we have seen in considering Lamartine, cancelling out the treatment of a woman as an individual reality, as a self-contained will to liberty. All this emerges from the history of Emma. Its effect upon the character of men we shall consider later.

Baudelaire (a contemporary, it is worth stressing) found Emma 'très-sublime ... en face de son petit horizon'.[48] Victor Brombert has similarly admired her dignified, *fantôme*-like figure when she overawes Justin, commanding our respect even as she swallows the arsenic.[49] But above all, Emma appears as the eternal feminine in her tragic relationship throughout her life with the male, presented by Flaubert in many forms, culminating in the very poison itself, the etymological sense of the word 'arsenic' being 'male'. 'Les bourgeois ne se doutent guère que nous leur servons notre cœur,'[50] wrote Flaubert to Feydeau. Flaubert's beloved sister Caroline died in childbed, that is, quite specifically as a result of the arrival of love, which is to say of the masculine in her life. So, just as certainly—and on the same day in the year—does Emma, if in a different way. In one case, the corruption has been physical infection resulting from fertility itself; in the other, the corruption is moral, following on a life which, for diverse reasons, has been spiritually sterile.

In this way did Flaubert exorcise the pain of the loss of Caroline. This is one of the causes of his famous remark: 'Madame Bovary, c'est moi.'

CHAPTER THREE

'Male and female created he them'

It is well documented that Flaubert initially planned to give the name Pyrrha to the heroine of his second great novel, the Carthaginian *Salammbô*. Pyrrha, the sole surviving woman from the classical flood, was, so Ovid tells us, the ancestress of modern 'stony-hearted' man. Thus Flaubert once expressly formulated an intention of recounting the history of an archetypal female figure. Comparisons with *Madame Bovary* and with contemporary epic poetry, humanitarian and encyclopaedic, come to mind. Laprade, in his *Psyché*, had for instance seen his heroine's labours as representing the trials of all humanity throughout history. The very name of Quinet's *mystère Ahasvérus* means 'all men' or 'Everyman', as in the title of the medieval English allegory.

After visiting North Africa in order to prepare his novel, Flaubert rejected Pyrrha and adopted instead a form of the Babylonian Venus for his heroine's name; this is again interesting in view of our conclusions concerning the presence of Venus within the character of Emma. Is the name Pyrrha of interest also for Emma? We know the importance of proper names for Flaubert, partly, I believe, because, nourished on Creuzer, he was aware of the varied etymologies, false and otherwise, that were given in antiquity to proper names of all kinds, aware also of their ambiguity which enabled him to fit them into his patterns of multivalent imagery. Thus two reasons for Flaubert's choice of the name Emma have already emerged: it is particularly Norman, having been a favourite name for Norman queens, and it is a near-anagram of the French word for the psyche, derived from the Latin *anima*. But the French inheritance shared by Charles and Emma is threefold. It is Celtic, Gallo-Roman, and also Germanic (leaving aside 'Egyptian', 'Ionian', and even 'Phoenician', of which we shall see more). The names Emma and Charles are of German origin. Charles is derived from the German *kerl* by way of the Latin *Carolus* and means, quite simply, 'male'. The name Emma, in origin, was the Embla whom Grimm mentions in his *Teutonic Mythology* as the first woman.

New perspectives are at once opened up, and our view of Emma as representing the evolution of conceptions of the human soul and of nature and the eternal feminine, all seen in terms of one another, is strengthened, particularly since, in Grimm, Freya the blue-eyed Northern nature goddess was also originally, like Athene–Isis–Venus Urania, an androgyne.

Emma is the name of Norman queens; Charles is even more prominent as a favourite name for French monarchs, as Montaigne mentions in his essay *Des noms.*[1] Furthermore, in nineteenth-century Normandy, its folklore well documented by, for instance, Flaubert's friends Alfred Maury and Amélie Bosquet,[2] the nature goddess of Northern climates in her most deadly form—white, icy-fingered, leader of the fatal hunt, the 'chasse Hennequin', implacable as winter itself—possessed among others the name Proserpine.

Now Emma, throughout the book, whitens her hands with lemon juice and bleaches her face with cold cream as her evolution proceeds. Isis, the nature-mother, so we find in the Plutarch Flaubert read so assiduously, 'is also winter'; Isis, we further note, 'is Proserpine'. There was, says Benjamin Constant, an Isis cult as far North in Europe as Silesia and Thuringia. In Gaul, Paris and Chartres were two notable cult centres. Thus, Athene–Isis, deity of the two Sais/Saez place-names (Egyptian and Norman) linked by the Celticists, is indeed present in Northern Europe—and not only grotesquely, as I first proposed her. In her capacity as nature-mother, Isis, so we are informed not only by Apuleius but by the hellenizing Herodotus, includes within her Demeter–Ceres. In all the classical traditions, Ceres as mother is also identified with the daughter, the maid Proserpine, for nature which gives birth also kills. 'On me dit une mère et je suis une tombe' are words attributed by Vigny[3] to the earth in both its capacities—as gentle bearer of vegetation and as cold indifferent planet spinning in the heavens in obedience to immutable laws. And Flaubert writes to Bouilhet as he struggles with his account of the modern nature-rite, the *Comices Agricoles,* the *nœud* of the whole novel: 'Cérès me poursuit. Quelle Proserpine!'[4] When Emma is lying on her deathbed, her own child will recoil in fear from her as from the wolf-witch of the winter-hunt herself: 'Oh! comme tu as de grands yeux, maman!'

How original is this search on the part of Flaubert in *Madame*

Bovary for certain *types* of person who shall sum up the evolving
ancestral experience of mankind while providing the necessary
'enveloppe' to tell a coherent story involving recognizable contemporary individuals? To answer the question it must first be noted
that, in the view of many readers both ancient and modern, Homer
himself was aware of allegorical and symbolic significances in his
work, though never mentioning them but presenting the interest
essentially in terms of the human aspects of his characters and
situations. The Abbé Le Bossu had written a commentary along
these lines as recently as 1675.[5] Fabre d'Olivet, in an influential essay
in 1813, had stressed the allegorical nature of Homer's work.
Flaubert records in a *Carnet* that Voltaire spoke of Homer as being
'entièrement symbolique'. Creuzer writes of the 'fil allégorique' which
seems to run in secret beneath the 'enveloppe extérieure' of the
Odyssey (noteworthy is the use of both 'fil' and 'enveloppe' by
Flaubert in regard to his own work). Now the great originality of
Flaubert among his contemporaries is that he also, on the surface of
his work, whatever depths he wished to convey on however many
levels, gives no explanation; all is implicit in imagery, situations, 'le
dessous'. When he proclaimed: 'Je veux qu'il n'y ait pas dans mon
livre . . . *une seule* réflexion de l'auteur,'[6] he was expressing a
principle, whereas Laprade, for instance, in his *Psyché* had explained
the allegory at every turn. To appreciate the aesthetic shortcomings
of such allegorical explanations, we do not perhaps have to look
further than Baudelaire's unfavourable review of the *Prométhée
délivré* written by Louis Ménard: 'Io, c'est à dire Madeleine ou Marie,
c'est à dire l'amour . . .'[7] I propose to show that, on the contrary,
Flaubert's novel, a consciously contrived successor to epic poetry,
aims at being equally allegorical but at expressing the allegory
secretly, in 'le dessous' of the narrative, using various devices which
we shall be seeing later.

'Il faut puiser aux sources primitives,' Hugo had urged in the
Préface de Cromwell, adding that in order to accommodate the
grotesque a modern Homer would necessarily be 'un Homère
bouffon'.[8] In Flaubert's early and overly allegorical, more simplistic
Smarh, it had been 'le grotesque' who won the woman, for he was 'le
vrai', while among Flaubert's better known remarks to Louise Colet
as he wrote *Madame Bovary* is his assertion that there were few things
in life he did not subject to his 'bouffonnerie'.[9] Flaubert-Saint
Polycarpe's low opinion of his own unheroic century being equally

well known, it is not surprising to us that he should take it as axiomatic that an epic set in the France in which he lived should indeed be 'bouffon', informed with the grotesque. The ancient world had believed that the last generation of heroes had fought and died around the walls of Troy. In modern French literature, Racine, 'honnête poète',[10] had exploited this conviction to tragically ironic effect in *Andromaque*, the plot of which concerns the sons of the heroes and the daughter of Helen. In *Madame Bovary*, Charles is similarly the inadequate offshoot of the Napoleonic French heroic age, just as Pyrrhus and Orestes are of Achilles and Agamemnon. For this matter, in Flaubert's own family, his doctor brother Achille was the evident inferior of their distinguished 'maître-homme'[11] father, whom, in the opinion of Sartre, he surely killed through bungling an operation. Certainly the medicine of the time was not particularly admired by Flaubert—one might even say it was loathed—and this is one of the themes of *Madame Bovary*. Can my comparison be justified by a reference anywhere to a son of one of the heroes? Yes, it can. Not only in the early versions does Charles at school read *Télémaque*,[12] Fénelon's seventeenth-century novel of the voyages of the son of Odysseus (under the tutelage of a disguised Athene–Minerva), the text similarly retains until the very late stage of the *mise au net* a quotation from Racine's *Phèdre* evoking Hippolytus, son of the hero Theseus.[13] Hippolytus slew no monsters nor rid the earth of any scourges, was sneered at by his father for his effeminacy and 'Orphism' in Euripides' play, and finally was killed, through a combination of angered goddesses, love-sick stepmother, and immoral nurse, as an innocent victim by a serpent-dragon sent out of the sea by Neptune at the request of a misinformed and over-hasty Theseus. The passage in question recounts his death and is famous in France as the 'récit de Théramène'. As Charles waits in the lane for the pre-arranged signal from Emma's father telling him whether or not she has accepted his proposal of marriage, he was to have recited it inwardly—as, until recently, most French schoolboys would have been able to do (and as Flaubert's *Dictionnaire des idées reçues* proclaimed that everyone should).[14] The shutter of the window bangs to, and Charles knows that his marriage to Emma will take place. With hindsight, we know that his own death and the closing down of his own coffin are as certain and irrevocable as hers.

In his final version, Flaubert suppressed the quotation from Racine, doubtless too specific a hint to us. This is not the first time, nor will it be the last, that we see Flaubert using a theme, motif, image for his own guidance, then removing it at the last minute. 'Le dessous' must retain its own mystery, but the guide-lines had been needed by the creative intelligence. For Hippolytus is certainly relevant to Charles. A solar hero, incarnation of pure light, his constellation is the mediterranean equivalent of the Northern Charles's Wain. Mention of him reminds us that, alongside the female Psyche, there is also a long tradition of visualizing the soul in masculine guise, as a series of pure heroes of the light in its most unsullied form, originally also androgynous. 'Le jour n'est pas plus pur que le fond de mon cœur' is the boast of Racine's Hippolyte, a line parodied at least once in Flaubert's correspondence.[15]

Now if Emma's androgynous nature as Athene–Psyche, possessed of extraordinary *candeur*, was stressed in our first sight of her, Charles's passive, gentle, sweet, rather 'effeminate' character was to have been highlighted even more in the *brouillons*. For it is possible to see in Charles, as we have seen in Emma, the evolution of a historical attitude. His name suggests the eternal masculine, set again in the North but heir to the multiple French tradition, with perhaps in the background Villon's complaint on the departure of French heroes: 'Mais où est le preux Charlemagne?' (especially in view of the handling of the syllables in 'Charbovary' when we first meet him). And, whereas in early life Emma's *candeur* is sullied by small lies at confession, Charles's great purity of heart endures, another fact commented on in the *brouillons*. Obtuse Charles may be, and difficult to admire (for he is in his very essence a grotesque anti-hero), but he is all love and all goodness until Emma's very deathbed, where Emma–Psyche at last recognizes the face of the god she has been seeking: 'Oui . . . , c'est vrai . . . , tu es bon, toi!' I would therefore postulate that, if the history of Emma evokes that of Psyche–Athene (pure spirit), Charles is cast alongside her in the role of Eros–Hippolytus (pure light). Thus, Creuzer's simplistic equivalences of soul and body, together with Hugo's ascription of 'sublime' and 'grotesque' to *La Belle et la Bête*, are rejected. Emma and Charles, feminine and masculine, are, as is the general human case, each in turn soul and body, spirit and matter, light and darkness, one to the other.

Sexual love quickens that part of us that we call the soul, but it is also concerned in paramount fashion with the physical and with life itself. There is no doubt that the Flaubert who wrote *Madame*

Bovary, to whom love brought venereal disease and whose sister had died in childbed, was terrified in the first place of love and secondly of nature. We find him wondering whether Louise Colet's own love for him is not a malediction visited upon her.[16] He urges her, repeatedly not to love him too deeply—'ça porte malheur à tous deux'.[17] People, his nephew-in-law for instance, seem born to cause one another greater misfortune.[18] And into all the ironies of love and nature in the histories of his near and dear he read a hidden destiny which had awaited them from the beginning, a pattern of revenge which might be discerned in a series of outward signs. 'Ma nièce est malade, elle vomit, comme son grand-père, comme sa mère; elle suivra peut-être le même chemin qu'eux; je m'y attends'[19] (Emma too was to vomit). Such an approach he applied to the lives of Emma and of Charles. 'N'as-tu pas vu que toute l'ironie dont j'assaille le sentiment dans mes œuvres n'était qu'un cri de vaincu, à moins que ce ne soit un chant de victoire?'[20] he cried to the uncomprehending Louise.

Sartre, while admitting that *Madame Bovary* is full of 'signes', dismisses them as gratuitous. He is quite wrong. The superstitious, haunted Flaubert who, before leaving for the East in 1849, was filled with foreboding at the sound of a barking dog ('j'envie les hommes forts qui à de tels moments ne remarquent pas ces choses'[21]) exorcized his terrors in the writing of *Madame Bovary*. 'Avec la *Bovary* finie, c'est l'âge de raison qui commence,'[22] he cries. For in this novel, in which he had wanted to reflect nature in its serenity and its complete lack of moral commentary or elucidation of human problems, he has striven from beginning to end, through ironic echoes and a rigorous if complicated and multivalent network of imagery, to impart to the lives of his main protagonists a subcurrent of inevitability, leading to their deaths which, as in a classical or Shakespearean tragedy, had been known before the writing began.

The word 'classical' is used here advisedly. It is of the highest importance for *Madame Bovary* in all the senses of the word—as applied to the works of the ancient 'classical' world of Greece and Rome, to the masterpieces of his own literature and to the productions of the consciously 'classical' French seventeenth century, all three of which Flaubert carefully studied. His own aim he clearly stated: 'être plus classique que les classiques et faire pâlir les Romantiques en dépassant leurs intentions. *Car c'est tout un.*'[23] Thus he envisaged returning to the 'procédés' of the ancient writers, though rejecting the direct imitation advocated by the Parnassian Leconte de Lisle (whom he admired) in the preface of his *Poèmes barbares* in 1852, and remaining in the classical tradition, as the sixteenth century had been able to do, but adding to this 'le sentiment moderne'.[24] What are the elements which Flaubert includes in *Madame Bovary* and which in his view represent the ancient classical writers as they do Romanticism? One answer could, I suggest, be the linking of a substructure of human destiny with a background presentation of the equally predestined workings of nature following equally ineluctable laws. *Madame Bovary* was without doubt intended to embody one of Flaubert's precepts: 'Le plus haut dans l'Art ... c'est d'agir à la façon de la nature. Aussi les très belles œuvres ... sont sereines d'aspect et incompréhensibles.'[25] Thus it would have 'une mine hautaine et classique'.[26]

For the underlying allegory perceived by the ancient authors—in, for example, Homer and in the myths cited by Creuzer, in particular also in those mentioned by the high priest of solar explanations to whom Creuzer constantly has recourse, Dupuis[27]—is most frequently one of the passage of the seasons, the apparent birth and death of the sun above the earth and the disappearance and renewal of vegetation upon the earth. These same phenomena were also seen as being at the heart of Northern myths by Grimm and by Flaubert's contemporaries. Thus the Romantics, in reviving and reproducing folklore as they did, were performing the same function as ancient authors in regard to their own nature myths. They were consciously not so much adding myths to their works as giving to the works as such the quality of the myth, making of each one a myth in itself, that is, a variation on the theme of man and nature. Goethe's *Werther* and Constant's *Adolphe*, for instance, had already provided modern examples in which the hero Werther in Goethe's novel and the heroine Ellénore in the work of Constant might have seemed to Flaubert to be solar-vegetation figures killed by love and its transmutation into cold, winter, and the death of the sun. Goethe's Charlotte (we note that the name is the feminine of Charles and has thus much the same sense as Emma and exactly that of Flaubert's sister Caroline) is at first a clear Ceres figure, dispensing bread and butter. With the introduction of Ossian and the moon, she becomes a snow queen of death, a Proserpine, and it is just before the winter solstice (22 December) that Werther, the 'just man', dies. When we come to the Constant novel, it is the woman who might have been seen as the victim. Constant was, of course, himself very learned on the subject of ancient religions, and his heroine Ellénore (whose name means 'light') is reminiscent of Northern queens of the May. Medievalists may recall the joyful refrain in *Le Roman de Guillaume de Dôle* addressed to the heroine Liénor: 'Voilà mai.' In Constant's novel, it is the hero Adolphe who (like Flaubert's Rodolphe) has the mythological wolf in his name—symbol of the sun in both its aspects, those of both summer and winter solstices, reminiscent of Ceres–Proserpine, the two aspects of the earth, with its attribute the moon. Now it is Adolphe who suggests that Ellénore, already sick, sit down outside on a winter's day. 'Le froid m'a saisie' are the words which herald her death and (however melancholy Adolphe may make his situation sound) his deliverance from her as 'la Nature sombre et silencieuse' carries out her pitiless work, 'd'un bras invisible'.[28] His love has killed her as the sun kills the dawn diurnally and as winter kills spring annually. Flaubert, in his own unpublished *nouvelle Novembre* had already introduced a solar equivalence when his hero's complete disappearance from the scene is described in the words: 'Ce n'est pas la belle saison.'[29]

In *Madame Bovary* there is no one representative victim. Both male and female are equally victims of love and each other, and this means victims of nature. There is in this novel both a king and a queen of the May (not forgetting again the French names Charles and Emma), both a hero of the pure light and a dawn maiden. Hero and heroine follow the destiny laid down by nature and—it must be added—by their own nature also. The effect of Emma–Psyche's contact with Eros is balanced by Charles–Hippolytus' treatment at the hands of Venus. An ironic view of existence, of love which brings death, that greatest irony of them all, as Flaubert describes it in his *Saint Antoine*, the irony of birth arising out of, indeed claiming, a preliminary death, traditionally had its foremost model in the apparent rising and setting of the sun, the untiring renewal of the solstices and of vegetation, the ceaseless succession of the constellations and the whirl of the heavens, the ironic guarantee ultimately of cosmic harmony. And not only is the inclusion of this background, as we have seen, Flaubert's declared intention, but he has adopted as one of the 'procédés' of the writers of antiquity an image which dominates the book, namely the *wheel*. Wheels turn endlessly throughout the book in countless forms—the wheels of carriages, of coaches, and of tilburies as of clocks, the gyrations of machinery as of a lampshade, a cottage spinning-wheel and Binet's lathe. Emma will die at the spring solstice, when the ancient lunar calendar began the year (certainly the calendar of Isis–Minerva–Venus–Proserpine). Death comes to Charles at the height of the summer, that is, at a point in the year corresponding with the death in Greece of Hippolytus (12 August). It was also the time when formerly in Egypt (with which Norman Celticists saw so many affinities) the old year died and the new incarnation of the sun, a new Hercules, set out on his way through the heavens. That Charles dies to be succeeded socially and metaphorically by another sun, Homais, was stressed in the *brouillons* by references to him in terms of 'le soleil d'Austerlitz'.[30] A different apotheosis was eventually adopted by Flaubert to describe the emergence of doctoring based upon drugs, sugar, and aerated waters in replacement of Charles's native docility to the processes of nature, Charles who (and this is an aspect of him as a grotesque hero which also underlines Homais's different approach) had started out in medical practice to 'exercer son art'.

Thus Emma and Charles are, side by side, representatives of suffering, dying, and eventually replaced solar-vegetation figures, visualized in two traditions as masculine and as feminine. Stress upon Charles as a composite figure is present from his first appearance, for this modern and by definition inadequate hero appears with a brand new imbecile form of headgear, 'd'ordre composite', the symbolic value of which is a commonplace of Flaubert criticism. What must be noted also is that the pathetic 'casque', as the schoolmaster derisively refers to it, is Flaubert's version of the old primary attribute of heroes in the old hero-sagas, the helmet, just as Emma's needle-case which she cannot at first find and is then so inexpert at using in our first meeting with her is his suggestion, as an 'Homère bouffon', of what has happened to the traditional heroine's workbasket.

Charles is brought to school by his flashy father, formerly an assistant Army surgeon. His names, Charles Denis Bartholomé, are interesting as those of Charles's progenitor. If the first represents the Northern Frankish element, Denis less obviously combines Egyptian with Celtic and Christian, the name having evolved from Dionysus, believed by Dupuis for instance to be the original of Saint Denis himself, accepted from Egypt as patron saint by the predominantly Celtic inhabitants of France who already nourished as part of their patrimony a cult of the human head. Dionysus–Saint Denis was beheaded and is thus represented as carrying his own head—with a host of other French saints, listed, for example, by Maury. This predominantly solar ancestry for Charles will prove interesting on a number of counts. The *signe* contained in the third name of Bovary *père*, Bartholomé, evokes the Roman element in the French inheritance. Another solar hero, another son of an illustrious father, is indicated, for the church of Saint Bartholomew, says Creuzer, stands where Esculapius' temple was formerly to be seen in Rome—Esculapius, doctor-son of Apollo, whose version of 'natural' medicine conformed so closely to Charles's own methods. Besides relying on nature and 'craignant de tuer son monde', Flaubert's Charles is even made to refer to a form of incubation, when 'la nuit porte conseil' is his advice on one occasion. In the early versions, a bust of Esculapius was to have stood on Charles's bookshelves,[31] until at the last moment Flaubert changed it to the better known and, in Charles's case, more grotesque Hippocrates. We have seen that one of the fascinations of studying Flaubert's various versions of *Madame Bovary* is to observe how he introduces motifs only to remove or exchange them and blur the edges. It seems again here that their presence has been more useful to Flaubert himself than intended for the reader, guides to himself in his battle with 'le style' and his preoccupation with 'le dessous'. As we have had occasion to note, the thought however still lingers within the text.

The importance that, in his pursuit of the 'procédés des anciens', Flaubert attaches to proper names extends to Denis–Dionysus and to the inheritance this denotes for Charles. Léon Bopp has noted in Charles a slight tendency to tippling.[32] In the early scenarios, he is shown to us as having even clearer connections with alcohol—he knows how to brew, he helps put wine in bottles.[33] The intention to establish the relationship was there from the beginning. But again Flaubert eliminates such direct, premature allusions to replace them with suggestions of a gradual, mounting development. Charles is the first answer provided by 'l'arrangement des choses' to Emma's longing for the 'félicité, passion, ivresse' she had read of in her books. Dionysus, the nature god, hunted down in *Saint Antoine* by bacchants and bacchantes alike, solar hero to the orphics, connected with the cult of Ceres–Proserpine, all these features are relevant, and we shall see them evolve within the character of Charles. Dionysus, also derisively androgynous in *Saint Antoine*, hailed in Sophocles' *Bacchantes* as equivalent to Eros himself, seen in the Christian tradition from the outset as a proto-Christ (the miracle at Cana of the water turning into wine is said by some historians to be identical with a piece of Dionysian magic-making) is also the Dionysus–Bacchus claimed by the sixteenth century and by André Chénier as a forerunner, and he is contained within the composite person of Charles–Eros. The latter, at the end of the novel and true to his character as a non-heroic figure in the ancient sense, that is, as a tearful modern product of the Christian religion and 'l'adoration des larmes',[34] ends by exonerating Rodolphe and thus by forgiving his enemy.

The rise of the theme of *ivresse* alongside that of the colour of wine and of blood is then relevant to Charles as to Emma. But Dionysus is the god of many forms, and he comes to Emma in the guise of other males and not just Charles alone. In this shape-shifting, Dionysus is equivalent not only to Eros but also to Hermes Psychopompus, beckoning and bearing the human soul on to its end, carrying out the will of the goddess, that is, of nature. The two candelabras which accompany Flaubert's Clésinger *Psyche and Eros* bear figures of on the one hand Psyche and on the other Hermes. For candles are consumed, the wheel of nature and of ineluctable time for ever turns. And Eros is Thanatos, as we have seen Venus to be Proserpine.

In *Madame Bovary* the protagonists undergo changes and these metamorphoses are reminiscent of successive human explanations of the secrets of nature, seen in particular in terms of masculine and feminine. Such techniques are essentially those of the ancient mysteries which related scenes from the beginning of the world to the present time, a design followed in more detail by Ovid's *Metamorphoses*. *Mystères* were a literary form named by Flaubert in 1846 among the genres he planned to write one day, and indeed many of the early works he had already written at the time had come into this category. Creuzer, whose volumes he read between 1848 and 1851, describes in detail the ancient mysteries as having begun in Sais (another reference to this key Egyptian/Norman name) and as having later been transported in modified form to Greece and, eventually, to Rome. The tradition was continued in the medieval mystery play, which presented similarly in an educative and initiatory form scenes from the Hebraic-Christian cosmologies. Quinet's *Ahasvérus*, model for the first version of *Saint Antoine*, provided a modern example; each is overtly entitled a *mystère*. *Madame Bovary*, an epic novel which, as I have sought to demonstrate, also proves to be an allegory, continues in many ways certain themes of *Saint*

Antoine, but they are now dissimulated, incarnate in modern characters and situations. They constitute the deep structure, 'le dessous', 'le fond', to which, throughout Flaubert's correspondence with Louise Colet, he ascribes the main part of his difficulty in writing. They account for 'le tissu minutieux' detected by Baudelaire[35] and are for Flaubert the essence of 'le style': 'Les bonnes œuvres sont celles où il y a pâture pour tous ... [les] artistes y verront le style ... [les] bourgeois ... y verront le sentiment.'[36] If the mind begins to boggle, Flaubert's correspondence again reassures us: 'C'est quelquefois si subtil que moi-même j'ai de la peine à me comprendre.'[37]

CHAPTER FOUR

'Savoir rouler une métaphore'

The central problem of criticism is to deduce the whole meaning
of a work through formal analysis.

It is time to look in more detail at the deep structure of Flaubert's
subtle and complex narrative and at his methods and techniques.
When composing *Madame Bovary*, the even flow constantly inter-
rupted by the untimely incursion into his mind of 'allégories
innombrables et métaphores incongrues',[1] he protests: 'Je suis gêné
par le sens métaphorique qui décidément me domine trop.'[2] From
the beginning, there was never any question of straightforward story-
telling—if such a thing exists—in this modern epic. Flaubert's
narrative proceeded deliberately on more than one level. He knew
and intended that his book should, like ancient epics in the view of
many critics in all ages, have a further sense or senses. In modern
prose, he maintained, there should be planes of perspective ('plans'),
often three or four.

To judge from the scenarios and rough drafts, Flaubert's method
was, in the early part of the novel, to start with a clear conception
which included deliberate references to certain objects that would
eventually be revealed as images—Emma's lamp and embroidery,
certain colours, dawns and sunsets, Charles's boots, animals, to
name but a few. At the same time, he accepted, as he wrote, other
metaphors which sprang unbidden from the unconscious, only to
examine them on revising the text, either for their fitness in the plan
already made or in an overall pattern towards which he groped. All
those which did not qualify as 'rigoureuses et justes'[3] he then firmly
expelled, extirpating all those, that is, which could not be assimilated
into the 'calcul' and 'ruses de style'[4] of the eventual unity of his
design, 'une machine si compliquée sous son apparence simple'.[5]
Similarly, a number of deliberately devised images, at first
consciously included, might be perceived also to be 'incongruous';
these were then modified in the light of newly accepted motifs,

41

spontaneous products of the creative imagination. The name
Rouault as Emma's and her father's family name, for instance, ousted
Lestiboudois (originally meant for them), for it fitted into the dominant image of the wheel which gradually grew with the novel. The
imagery developed with the writing; this is what Flaubert meant by
being able to 'penser le style' only pen in hand.[6]

Flaubert rarely speaks of symbols, except as a joke; too many
other writers had been and were doing so. He was aware of contemporary attitudes, and admitted that he had once been
enthusiastic for 'les Micheletteries' and 'les Quinetteries',[7] for
example. But study of the past had convinced him of the cliché
nature of so many of them. A notable and serious use of the word
'symbole' is to be found however in an early letter referring to his
young niece's baptism. Flaubert writes: 'En contemplant tous ces
symboles insignifiants pour nous, je me faisais l'effet d'assister à
quelque cérémonie d'une religion lointaine, exhumée de la pous-
sière. C'était bien simple et bien connu, et pourtant je n'en revenais
pas d'étonnement.'[8] The 'frisson historique' which Flaubert referred
to elsewhere as a modern characteristic[9] is relevant to the whole
approach to religions and their development discernible in 'le
dessous' of *Madame Bovary* and reminiscent of *Saint Antoine*. The
Notes de voyage provide another example. When did the habit of
placing evergreen upon tombs begin? he wonders.[10] Traditions, even
superstitions, are for Flaubert subjects less for scoffing (until
Bouvard et Pécuchet) than for investigation.

In designating figurative expressions, Flaubert's habitual terms
were *image* and *couleur* (near-synonymous for him). In particular, he
talked about metaphors. 'Bonnes métaphores!' he wrote encourag-
ingly to Ernest Feydeau as the latter was embarking on his second
novel. The whole art of writing might be described as the elaboration
of a metaphor. The only flowers to be gathered in the life of a dedicated writer, in which the adventures consist of sentences, are indeed
metaphors. Flaubert was well aware, as we have seen, that there is in
all works a 'poétique insciente',[11] arising from factors within the
psyche of which the artist is not necessarily conscious, just as the
reader is affected by aspects of a work without knowing that anything
is going on. 'La littérature est l'art de se jouer de l'âme des autres,'
Valéry would later say. Flaubert's aim, like that of the poet, was to
render these processes conscious for the writer. Each work has its
own 'poétique', which, as it proceeds, 'il faut trouver'.[12] Once found, it

must consciously be elaborated and without fear of exaggeration, provided that the exaggeration is harmonious. Molière, in *Monsieur de Pourceaugnac*, filled the whole stage with syringes, exulted Flaubert,[13] for all the truly great have always exaggerated. In his own case—and highly successfully—he filled *Madame Bovary* with endlessly revolving circular motions and gyrations: of the sun and uninterrupted swirl of the heavens as of an ironic fate, for which, in *King Lear*, 'the wheel is come full circle', Edgar's lament of recognition, is the fitting classical image. Yet never is there a suggestion of melodrama, only of the pity and relentlessness of it all, this universe in which everything is designed for the greater harmony of the whole regardless of the individual or the detail. Likewise, the poet inserts all manner of 'ruses' which will lure the reader along ways of thought deliberately planned ahead for him but hidden. The important series of images relating to embroidery and spinning (relevant not only to the traditional workbasket of the heroine, but also to Minerva, goddess of spinning and weaving, as we shall see) come into this category. 'Prendre garde de le faire trop haut,'[14] Flaubert inserted above the line in an early scenario, reminding himself to beware of making the theme too obvious. This is a specific and therefore highly important indication of Flaubert's conscious method of composition and of his careful planning of elements to be included in 'le dessous' before serious writing began. In his review of *Madame Bovary*, Sainte-Beuve wrote that from beginning to end Flaubert had done exactly what he wanted.[15]

Such a strong element of the conscious diminishes the relevance for Flaubert of some of the French 'new criticism', for instance of the concept of 'oneiric literature' in which Gaston Bachelard has categorized writers having a highly metaphorical style. For Bachelard, recurrent images in a work of literature are indications of psychic 'hantises' on the part of the writer, the images in the whole work forming a 'synthesis' which is apparently 'artificial', that is, conscious,while being in fact, so he holds, 'natural', that is, 'unconscious' (*L'Eau et les rêves*).[16]

But a writer's initial conception of his work can prescribe from the outset the conscious contrivance of a 'synthesis' of images, as we have seen to be the case with Flaubert. This original network can then be enriched in the process of composition by further patterns underlying different, unprompted imagery, also flowing—but now unconsciously—from the *idée mère* with which the work began. A

highly conscious artist will recognize most if not all of these new sets
of images, and may deliberately adopt them and develop them
further within the work, superimposing, interweaving or even
exchanging them for what he had intended.

Bachelard did not write about Flaubert, but it is similarly
questionable whether the brilliant study of Flaubert by Bachelard's
disciple Professor Jean-Pierre Richard is always strictly relevant to
Flaubert's creative processes as seen at work in the actual writing of
the novels.[17] For instance, where Flaubert's use of images connected
with water is concerned, Richard's interpretation evokes Flaubert's
personal,   largely   unconscious   preoccupations,   notably—so
frequently do images connected with love refer to liquidity and
fluidity—a near-condemnation of love as amounting to a dissolution
of the being. This is most valuable, adding a new dimension to
Flaubert's undoubted fear of love that I have referred to in an earlier
chapter. Demorest, upon whose pioneer study of Flaubert's figurative expressions Richard draws, has shown, however, that it is largely
in the 'spontaneous' productions, the correspondence and the rough
drafts of novels, that these images of love as fluidity occur, and it is
from these texts that many of Richard's own quotations are taken.[18]
Yet, if we compare the rough drafts and the finished works of art,
Madame Bovary for instance, it is interesting to see how very many of
Flaubert's 'spontaneous' references to water and insubstantiality
have been suppressed by him in the process of correcting.

Thus, though it is certain that Flaubert feared love as something
which would dissolve and prevent the development of that part of his
being which produced works of art, yet clearly water imagery had a
special significance for the conscious artist also, and much of it he
deliberately retained. In *Madame Bovary* as in *Salammbô*, in
L'Éducation sentimentale and in *Hérodias*, references to water are
present for their relevance to themes. Léon Bopp asks, with regard to
Madame Bovary, whether it rains every day in Rouen;[19] he might well
reiterate his question for Paris in *L'Éducation sentimentale*, over
which, to quote Brombert, a 'steady drizzle falls'.[20] In both, allusions
to humidity form part of a specific design. Not only is there stress on
the Heraclitean damp souls, 'les mousses de moisissure de l'âme'[21]
which we have seen to be the declared subject of the Northern epic
which is *Madame Bovary*; there is also the relationship between
moisture and the 'female' element in nature, which in *Salammbô*, in a
context of ancient religions, Flaubert will find it possible to indicate

overtly but which is also present in his novels about modern France. In this respect, Richard might have referred to his master Bachelard, who notes the relationship between humidity and the feminine in the works of certain German poets, though in keeping with his usual method he sees the equivalence not as the result of deliberate calculation on the part of the writers but as an unconscious surfacing of some archetypal awareness. In Flaubert's works, alongside the contribution made by the unconscious to any process of composition, the ultimate effect, as we have seen, is as deliberately contrived as he is capable of making it. Humidity signifies matter— 'la matière humide', as it is described in the first *Saint Antoine*: in other words, moisture has a definite relationship with the nature goddess who is discernible behind his women characters and whose 'attributes' and significance he had carefully studied and then (sometimes after recognition) consciously reproduced and introduced.

The word 'attributes' is important. For, just as in ancient and religious representations of god, hero, saint, attributes are included to indicate identity—Isis' crescent horns and moon-disc, Ceres' wheat stalks, Venus' roses and doves, Hercules' club, or St Catherine's wheel—so Flaubert includes details with the same intent, namely, to call our attention to an identity at hand, otherwise hidden from us beneath the surface of the natural as well as human world. As a hint to us how to read these details, of whose existence he perhaps by this point in the novel expects us to be aware, if only dimly, Flaubert inserts in Emma's latest dream of Léon the sentence: 'Il se perdit, comme un dieu, sous l'abondance de ses attributs.' And so it is with Emma, Charles, Rodolphe, Homais, and the adjuncts with which Flaubert has connected them.

In no aspect of his work is Flaubert's study of ancient writers and his imbibing of Creuzer's theories concerning the symbolism of the religions of antiquity more important. Flaubert deliberately went in search of what he described as 'types' in his concern to continue, knowingly, in the line of what he believed to be 'la tradition'. 'Il faut toujours monter ses personnages à la hauteur d'un type . . . tâcher d'écrire pour l'éternité,' he would later write to Feydeau.[22] His formal preoccupation with the expression of these types through imagery is thus an integral part of his subject-matter. 'Forme' and 'fond' are indivisible, as he always maintained.

Flaubert, then, distrusted the unconscious, the 'bals masqués de l'imagination'.[23] He held Apollo, not Dionysus, in regard. Flaubert quoted Bouilhet as saying that inspiration should be induced and not submitted to[24] (there is resemblance to Mallarmé in that sentence). The carefully thought out 'conception' of the whole book became a configuration of ideas, each of which, according to an approved precept of the eighteenth-century writer Buffon whom Bouilhet and Flaubert discovered to have shared their own views, must be expressed by an image. The immediate surface effect to be aimed at is plasticity, held to be the strongest element in art, an opinion not surprising in a *visuel* like Flaubert, whose injunctions to another writer included the advice: 'Emplissez-vous la mémoire de statues et de tableaux.'[25] But within the narrative there is, he constantly maintains, as we have seen, 'le dessous', the thought which he rendered 'plastic' in the finished work. Creuzer's many pages on how to decipher the attributes and *signes* in ancient figurative representations (wheels, flowers, doves, triangles, whips, veils, colours, animals, and so on—the list is very long), together with Flaubert's own comments on pictures seen in Italy (wondering for instance at the significance of touches of colour—blue and red—and assuming also irony and foreshadowing to be deliberately intended in the corpse-like babe seen in German nativities)[26]—all these help us understand what he meant, for they suggested to him his own iconographical and attributive method of narration. When, with his mother, he visited the 1851 exhibition in London, he noted in detail the insignia on the Chinese exhibits and was sorry not to be able to identify the attributes of a Chinese god.[27] Louis Bouilhet's lines on a 'langage des choses naturelles' which the primitive poet knew how to read, reminiscent for us of Baudelaire's *Correspondances*, the contemporary 'Orphic' desire to return to what the poet Soumet designated as 'cette langue primitive, révélée à l'homme par Dieu même' and in which 'tout est symbolique',[28] all these are relevant. Flaubert, when reading the first volume of Stendhal's *Le Rouge et le Noir* in 1845, had wondered if the language of this 'esprit distingué', whose style was certainly 'français', was really 'le vrai style, ce vieux style, qu'on ne connaît plus maintenant'.[29] Its attainment was Flaubert's own preoccupation, as it was that of the poets, his contemporaries. But for Flaubert, it was by 'malices' and 'ruses' issuing from the head and not the heart that the modern writer could reach it. 'Soyons des virtuoses. La naïveté de nos jours est une chimère,'[30] he concluded, having just studied also the highly allusive style of the ancient poet Perses.

The result in *Madame Bovary* is the deliberately contrived, complicated substructure of recurrent images and themes I have described. Images often overlap, wheels with lamps with colours with liquidity and so on; all, however complex the network, are necessary to deepen the significance of the narrative. 'Vous heurtiez la poétique interne,'[31] protested Flaubert when the printer Laurent-Pichat tried to remove some of them—a candelabra, a snake—which seemed to him, as to Maxime du Camp and the *Revue de Paris* in general, to be well-wrought but superfluous surface details. I shall attempt to show what he meant, but first let it be stressed again that it is perfectly possible to say—and quite often—when Flaubert's effects are deliberate. Two checks are available to us. One is purely textual—the unity of the imagery, of the patterns which recurrent motifs (the wheel, the web, water, animals, sun and moon, to name but a few) form on both a literal and figurative level. The other is there in particularly advantageous form in the case of Flaubert, namely the rough drafts and scenarios to which I have already had frequent occasion to refer. The alterations which they contain prove that in Flaubert's narrative an image is not present for its own sake but for the pattern to which it belongs—or indeed, as I have said, for a number of patterns, a feature of Flaubert's imagery being that it is so frequently polyvalent. 'Ma cervelle me semble petite pour embrasser d'un seul coup d'œil cette situation complexe,' he groaned when writing the *Comices*, 'le nœud dont tout dépend.'[32]

In *Madame Bovary* imagery has a further function, that of expressing and emphasizing the irony which, for Flaubert, is the chief component of the language of nature as of life, and which led him to formulate his aim in *Madame Bovary* as 'l'acceptation ironique de l'existence et sa refonte plastique et complète dans l'art'.[33] Motifs echo ironically those that have preceded, presenting a picture of an unseen force which is not only indifferent—'comme ça se fout de nous, la Nature!'[34]—but vengeful in the face equally of Emma's energy and Charles's passivity. Both may be victims, but both also, wittingly, have offended—as Priam, in giving his support to Paris and Helen, abetted them in their offence against Jupiter the hospitable, and died at the foot of his statue in Virgil's *Aeneid*. The Latin poem had been read by Flaubert in 1846 with tremendous enthusiasm; the punishment which, in Virgil's poem, lies waiting in the background is commented on by Creuzer. It is highly relevant to Flaubert's view of nature and to his narrative method in *Madame Bovary*. In the grip of the pain which inspired him to tell his story in the destiny-haunted manner of the ancients, Flaubert exclaimed that he would never seek to justify human nature. Yet there must not be hatred either, in the narrative of this man who, in his private life, could say 'moi qui déteste la nature'[35] but for whom as artist the task was to suppress such feelings: 'Pas de haine! Peignons! peignons!... mais des tableaux complets, le dessus et le dessous.'[36]

In commenting upon Flaubert's figurative expressions, Don Demorest in his pioneer work saw 'un besoin classique de la symétrie',[37] and this, I suggest, is precisely Flaubert's essential method for conveying irony. The dazzling white sugar at La Vaubyessard will be balanced by the white powder of the arsenic which kills Emma (an equivalence between sugar and poison is established throughout the book and in the rough drafts Emma actually eats the arsenic 'à mêmè comme du sucre'[38]); Emma and Charles chatting before the kitchen door at Les Bertaux beneath an umbrella upon which the thaw is gently dripping will be balanced by her conversation with Léon at the beginning of their fatal affair— now menacing 'éclairs' illuminate the sky; as Charles enters the farm yard at Les Bertaux, he loves the sound of 'le coq qui chantait sur le mur', and he will hear it again as he walks in her funeral procession. Moreover, it is the attribute of Esculapius, ironically, the patron of doctors, whose relevance for Charles we have already had occasion to note.

The underlying metaphorical patterns chosen for treatment in the following pages all have particular reference to Flaubert's handling of traditional (and this includes ancient) conceptions of masculine and feminine, that is to say, as I have sought to show, of man in his relations with nature. They are to be seen on two levels. The ancient 'Orphic' style, Flaubert could have learned from Creuzer, consisted of the very allegory and symbolism which came so naturally to him. Before passing to the detailed imagery which constitutes the symbolism woven around the main subject, that of the passage through life and history of two representative human souls, let us consider this general allegorical level. In *Madame Bovary,* the central metaphor emerges as marriage, as in the ancient nature mysteries. In these, a marriage between two representative figures reenacted the 'mystic' union of the 'two principles', of masculine and feminine, that is, also, of heaven and earth (as Saint Antoine's vision had clearly shown), of heat and moisture (as overtly indicated in *Salammbô*), and, by extension, of spirit and matter.

Once it is registered that, as we saw in Chapter Three, Emma and Charles are composite figures, such an incarnation of one of the two 'principles' (as seen in their very names), then all the mystic marriages which used to be enacted in the mysteries become relevant, as I shall show. Alongside that of Eros and Psyche, there were the marriages of Zeus and Hera, Osiris and Isis, Dionysus and Ariadne, Venus and Adonis, with finally in Rome Liber–Libera, that is to say, Bacchus and Proserpine. Pages of illustrations of these allegorical mystic marriages appear in Creuzer. I shall argue that in *Madame Bovary* they start with Egypt and evolve at least as far as Rome. Then, as the Christian inheritance of this classical background, Emma's modern initiation into religious life at the convent school had also had associations with a type of mystic marriage: 'Les comparaisons de fiancé, d'époux, d'amant céleste et de mariage éternel qui reviennent dans les sermons lui soulevaient au fond de l'âme des douceurs inattendues.' Later, when sexual relations in the form of Charles, the young Léon (platonically) and both episodes with Rodolphe have failed her, Emma turns to religion and would like to become a saint. She murmurs on her *prie-dieu* the words she had uttered to her lover. Book in hand, she reclines on a divan in her room, evidently aping some visual illustration of one of her literary or religious models, role-playing being, as modern psychology maintains, a means adopted by the psyche to free itself from physical circumstances and constriction, absurd though Emma's efforts may seem. In her exaggerated dedication of herself to good works (her mania for knitting garments for orphans, instead of doing the household mending), Emma is visibly seeking to emulate the royal saint whose name she bears. But, just as her exaggerated aspirations to impersonate Athene–Minerva lead to her punishment, so the saint it is in fact vouchsafed to her to resemble is another Egyptian who came to Normandy and settled on the hill in Rouen which bears her name and which is mentioned several times by Flaubert, notably in the description of the city as Emma enters it one Thursday morning in the old yellow coach. This saint's name, moreover, is borne by the old farm worker, Catherine Leroux, whose chief preoccupation, despite her resemblance to the animals, is her source of transcendence, leading her to offer her gold medal to the priest in return for masses to be said for her soul (Catherine's aspirations show her to be very like Emma, that is, another representative of an eternal characteristic, instead of her complete converse, as is often thought). Like Emma, the saint in question, Catherine of Alexandria, also read

books, won prizes for learning, experienced a mystic marriage, and
was sentenced to torture on the wheel, the dominant image in
Madame Bovary, as we have seen. In an early version of Emma's
return from Rouen to Yonville, she suffers 'comme si les roues de la
voiture eussent été celles d'un engrenage pour la supplicier'.[39]

The episode of Emma's aspiration to saintliness prepares us for
the intimations of a possible mystic marriage which occur again to
Emma on her deathbed, when she implants upon 'le corps de
l'Homme-Dieu le plus grand baiser d'amour qu'elle eût jamais
donné'. Throughout her life she had longed to be exalted, transported, utterly and entirely 'dans un grand baiser'; her illusion and
belief in the love of a man who should also be a god, her desire for
transcendence, for release from the flesh, for a 'volupté plus haute',
have not dimmed. Emma is no more a saint then she is an artist, and
the borderline between religious and sensual ecstasy is particularly
indeterminate in such an 'esprit positif'. Yet the aspiration is there.
Emma–Psyche has, like Apuleius' heroine pricked by one of Eros'
arrows, fallen in love with love himself, and to the end he is her quest.
It is not irrelevant here to note that in early Christian art the pictorial
representations of Psyche and Eros signified the Christian soul in
search of God, as Flaubert knew from Creuzer and from his own visit
to the Roman catacombs. These Christian undertones become particularly important in the later works, in which Flaubert's
preoccupation with his own century stands revealed as the fundamental explanation of his interest in the history of religions.

In *La Tentation de saint Antoine*, women recount to the saint how
in their dreams they had seen 'des dieux qui les appelaient'. Maria in
Novembre wonders where in the modern world are the gods of the
ancients: 'plus de Bacchus, plus d'Apollons.'[40] Salammbô cries out to
Mâtho: 'Moloch, tu me brûles!'[41] The theme of a woman who longed
to be loved by a god was one which attracted Flaubert over a long
period (indeed, he had first met it in his youthful reading of
Montaigne). Emma is no exception. Charles seems to her incapable
of initiating her into 'tous les mystères'. Only on her deathbed does
she recognize him as Charles–Eros, gazing at her with tenderness
such as she had never seen: 'Oui . . . , c'est vrai . . . , tu es bon, toi!'
Instead, she has sought to find elsewhere in other men the face of the
god of love—in the young Léon, to whom in the firelight her gaze,
when they first met, turned as to the sun-god himself; in Rodolphe,
whom she certainly addressed in terms of idolatry and even as good:

'Tu es bon!', 'il est si bon'; in Lagardy the tenor, who seemed to her 'l'incarnation de l'amour même' (here Flaubert makes 'le dessous' explicit); finally in Léon again, willing herself to visualize the handsome feeble boy 'tel un dieu'.

Behind all these situations, the mystic marriages peer through. I have already shown the presence of Psyche and Eros both at Charles's first meeting with Emma and finally at her death. Thirty-five references to the word *âme*, used in a traditional idealist sense, occur in the course of the novel, culminating, after all the contacts with the material and with appearance which constitute her story, in the terrifying description of her end: 'Sa poitrine aussitôt se mit à haleter rapidement. La langue tout entière lui sortit de la bouche; ses yeux . . . à la croire déjà morte, sans l'effrayante accélération de ses côtes, secouées par un souffle, furieux, comme si l'âme eût fait des bonds pour se détacher.'

All the references to the etymological sense of *l'âme* (as of 'psyche'), namely, *le souffle*, which have been interspersed throughout the novel now too are gathered here into a final significance, along with those occasions when Emma has choked for breath, gasped for air. 'Je ne sais pas où l'âme commence, où le corps finit . . . tout est lié,' Flaubert had declared. And 'j'étouffe', 'elle étouffait', have constituted a refrain recurrent throughout the novel at those key moments when it seemed to Emma that the body and all matter were triumphing over her struggling essence. In springtime at Tostes, 'elle eut des étouffements', 'elle suffoquait'. In Homais's shop when Emma is terrified that Binet will reveal that he had seen her in the early morning, the chemist's wife marvels at her: 'Comme vous respirez fort!' Then there is Emma pressed by Charles to take one of Rodolphe's apricots; Emma wishing to leave the theatre so as to talk to Léon whose 'souffle' in her hair as he stood behind her has reawakened her; Emma arriving at la mère Rolet's house ('J'étouffe'); Emma hearing that Léon has not brought the money, feeling madness coming upon her ('elle haletait') when suddenly the thought of Rodolphe 'lui avait passé dans l'âme'. At Guillaumin's house, she arrives 'tout essoufflée', as formerly on her morning visits to Rodolphe. 'Son sein haletait' as she talks to Binet. Rushing home from her disappointing last interview with Rodolphe, 'elle ne souffrait que de son amour, et sentait son âme l'abandonner pour ce souvenir. . . . Elle haletait à se rompre la poitrine.' On her deathbed, 'J'étouffe' heralds the period when the poison takes effect. Later, 'à chaque souffle de sa poitrine' she seems to be improving, until another instance of the word 'haleter' introduces the final fearful evocation of a soul wishing to have done with the body.

Another recurring image connected with the Psyche substructure of *Madame Bovary* is the *papillon*, a further sense of the Greek word *psyche* and meaning in French both moth and butterfly. Creuzer comments in particular on its original sense as the 'papillon de nuit, amant de la lumière' whose ' noble instinct' is also 'funeste et cause sa mort'. The moths fluttering around the candle as Charles receives his Latin lessons from the old *curé* will prefigure for us his own as well as Emma's story when, looking back over the whole book, we see it as part of a pattern of recurrent references. At these lessons Charles's initiation into medicine takes place, leading to his and Emma's whole destiny, including his very meeting with her. Yellow sun-coloured butterflies are then chased by Djali, as Emma, who has realized that she is imprisoned in her particular marriage, wanders with him among the ruins, the nettles, and the foxgloves. In the famous scene when her burning wedding bouquet releases into the night sky a swarm of black moths, the theme of her inevitable death (and, in some eyes, damnation) has entered the stage. The white butterflies evoked by the peasant women's bonnets at the *Comices*, their wings set in motion by a 'coup de vent', say something of their expectations of a form of exaltation as they stand 'bouche bée' in this gathering (in early versions of the initial scenes in the novel Emma was to have worn one of these winged bonnets). They are echoed when further white butterflies, formed by the torn fragments of her letter of renunciation to Léon and signifying the end of all her resolutions and the extinction of her virtue, are scattered by the wind among heads of red clover in full bloom, colour of the blood which she will vomit on her deathbed, blood (in the literal and figurative sense) from which the fluttering soul, as Flaubert's whole story stresses, is inseparable, colour also of the sunset and therefore of the male.

Finally, there is the Emma–Psyche–Minerva who figured in Flaubert's early plan for the novel, seated 'avec sa lampe et ses broderies'.[42] Psyche's lamp which, overwhelmed with curiosity, she lit in the night in order to see the forbidden face of the god of love, occurs in Emma's story at moments when she too is seeking information about love in the reading-matter which contributes so importantly to the direction of her life. First, when reading at night in the convent, 'l'abat-jour du quinquet' above her head is combined with wheel imagery and indeed, specifically—in foreshadowing—a *fiacre*; at an evening party spent with the Homais, the theme again overlapping with the wheel, Emma 'faisait tourner machinalement l'abat-jour de la lampe', while Léon read aloud to her from the Romantic poets; thirdly, upon the departure of Léon, when life for Emma has become 'de tous côtés nuit complète', Charles awakens from sleep with a start: 'et c'était le bruit d'une allumette qu'Emma frottait afin d'allumer la lampe', so as to be able to read. This time the theme is openly connected with the embroidery of the preparatory scenario: 'mais il en était de ses lectures, comme de ses tapisseries, qui, toutes commencées, encombraient son armoire; elle les prenait, les quittait, passait à d'autres.' Emma is ready for experience with Rodolphe.

A lamp had also been mentioned when Emma, actuated in springtime by vague spiritual longings, wishing to be consumed in any devotion 'pourvu qu'elle absorbât son âme et que l'existence entière y disparût', makes her way, automaton-like, to church, only to be offered 'les remèdes de la terre'. The lamp burning on the altar had consisted of 'une mèche de veilleuse'; a 'veilleuse de porcelaine' is interestingly shedding a circle of light on the ceiling as Emma, pretending to sleep, dreams of another vehicle—the 'malle-poste' which she believes is to carry her away with Rodolphe and which is based again on her literary reminiscences. Charles, dreaming in his turn about the future of his daughter, sees her characteristically in terms of the young Emma, still essentially unchanged for him. She would work 'à la lumière de la lampe' and would embroider slippers for him (this future worker in a cotton mill—oh irony!). She and Emma would be taken for 'les deux sœurs'—the remark will later prove to have further significance.

Among other interpretations of the Psyche myth, summarized by Creuzer and perhaps contributing to the genesis of Flaubert's work, is that of Thoelaeius: 'L'histoire d'Éros et de Psyché est un mythe moral qui a pour but de représenter les dangers courus par la foi conjugale.' The two archetypal figures of the first married couple, Hera–Juno and Zeus–Jupiter, are grotesquely reenacted in *Madame Bovary* by the Bovary parents—Bovary *père* in pursuit of 'toutes les gotons du village' resembling the Jupiter of *Saint Antoine*, who has 'perdu [ses] cheveux sur tous les lits',[43] not to speak of being an 'homme à ne rien respecter', and la mère Bovary recalling Hera in her exclusive attention to the son who is very much her sole creation, as

Hephaestus was reported to have been born to Hera alone. The heavy-footed stout-booted Charles evokes Hera's son in little else than this, perhaps, until he also becomes a betrayed husband, betrayed moreover by his wife in her role as Venus, as Hephaestus had been. At the Château de La Vaubyessard, where the desire and possibility of unfaithfulness first came to Emma, she not only wore the roses of Venus as she gazed at herself in the mirror, but 'ses yeux noirs semblaient plus noirs'. In *Saint Antoine*, Venus Anadyomene, surrounded by roses, also looks at her reflection in a mirror: 'ses prunelles glissent langoureusement sous ses paupières un peu lourdes'[44] (reminiscent also of Emma–Venus when we first saw her at Les Bertaux), and from her exudes a glow which Emma will again recall in her period of happiness: 'quelque chose de subtil qui vous pénétrait se dégageait même des draperies de sa robe et de la cambrure de son pied.' At the corner of the mouth of Flaubert's Venus Anadyomene—a connecting link in his thought with the Psyche theme—there hovers a butterfly.

But it is Emma who becomes representative of the body and of matter for the pure soul that is Charles, although in his worship of her as extra-terrestrial he cannot see this. The situation is prefigured in the slippers she embroiders for him and of which he is so proud, feet and footwear being in Flaubert's creative works equivalent to the 'clous de nos bottes'[45] which, as he remarks in the correspondence, tie us to the earth. Saint Antoine, wishing to escape from all connection with the earth, cries out: 'Je voudrais ne pas tenir à la terre,—même par la plante de mes pieds!'[46] In *L'Éducation sentimentale*, Flaubert later succeeds in investing the occasionally visible 'pointe du pied' of Madame Arnoux with all the attractions of the flesh and of the eternal feminine. Throughout *Madame Bovary*, a contrast is in question between heads and feet, one which will be summed up most effectively (because most explicitly) in *Hérodias*. The plaster curé's missing foot, Charles's boots that are 'bien assez bonnes pour la campagne', the *pied bot* which Charles cannot cure, Emma's 'bottines' covered with 'la crotte des rendez-vous', all (and others) are linked with recalcitrant matter, with the 'choses de ce monde'. This is not surprising in a novel which, as we have seen—an aspect of the multivalent story of Psyche and Eros—is a dialogue between Minerva and Dionysus, allegorical products in turn of the head and of the foot of the father of the gods.

'Mettre un chien dans la maison,' Flaubert instructs himself in an

early scenario.[47] Emma is given a greyhound by a satisfied patient
and names it after the pet goat belonging to Hugo's 'Egyptian'
heroine in *Notre-Dame de Paris*. It will accompany her on lonely
walks, even as the Isis of specifically Egyptian mythology was
accompanied by her dog Anubis in her search for the missing body
of her husband Osiris, destroyed by Typhon, the god of evil. Emma is
disappointed in her marriage, which we now perceive to have had
some reference to the mystic union of Isis with Osiris, 'le taureau du
soleil', whose name, as we shall see later, can be heard grotesquely in
Charles's surname. She too feels robbed as she roams with her dog in
a manner reminiscent of Flaubert's very description of the Isis of his
first *Saint Antoine*, dropped in 1856 when the comparison might
perhaps have been feared to be too obvious to some readers,
restored in the final version of 1874.[48] The yellow butterflies chased
by the dog, whose movements, we are told, reflect those of Emma's
thoughts, connect the incident with the Psyche and eternal feminine
themes on the one hand (yellow, we remember, being the colour of
the dawn and therefore of the female, especially in Egyptian
mythology); 'coquelicots', both by their colour (that of blood, the
sunset, and the male) and by their poison, foreshadow her certain
death. The passage contains many other corroboratory elements,
and a notable example of the overlapping of imagery is provided by
the poppies already mentioned, for these were one of the attributes
of that other nature-mother, Demeter–Ceres, at whose modern
festival, the *Comices Agricoles*, Flaubert will, as part of his preparation for another mystic marriage, later point to the juxtaposition
within Emma of both deities.

This he achieves through a confrontation of Emma and other
attributes of the goddesses, this time animals. We are told of her: 'Son
profil était si calme que l'on ne devinait rien ... Ses yeux aux longs cils
courbes regardaient devant elle'; then, later, we read: 'les vaches ...
ruminant lentement, clignaient leurs paupières lourdes.' We are
reminded first of the traditional portraits of Isis in hieratic pose,
always in profile, and secondly of her crescent horns (in the early
versions there had been many more references to cows, notably at a
moment during Emma's wanderings with Djali, when she is
frightened by 'une vache qui passe la tête par-dessus la haie',[49] a hint
to us much too crude to be retained). Alongside this juxtaposition,
there is a reference to the mares. Like Emma, 'elles restaient
paisibles, allongeant la tête et la crinière pendante'. Already at

school, had not Emma been depicted in terms similarly evocative? She had stopped short, 'et le mors lui sortit des dents'. Demeter the mare-headed goddess is brought to mind. The allusion here is to another mystic marriage, that of the earth-goddess Demeter–Ceres and Zeus–Jupiter in the person of Rodolphe. During the affair between them, Emma will be described in terms of a product of the earth itself:

Jamais Madame Bovary ne fut aussi belle qu'à cette époque . . . Ses con-voitises, ses chagrins, l'expérience du plaisir et ses illusions toujours jeunes, comme font aux fleurs le fumier, la pluie, les vents et le soleil, l'avaient par gradations développée, et elle s'épanouissait dans la plénitude de sa nature.

At the same time, Rodolphe's surname Boulanger is in fact one of the names of Jupiter, being a direct translation of the Latin *Pistor*, given to him by the Romans following an incident in which he pacified their enemies during a siege by throwing them loaves of bread. From this mystic marriage, Proserpine was born; a new Emma will emerge from the relationship with Rodolphe. 'Cérès me poursuit. Quelle Proserpine!',[50] Flaubert wrote to Bouilhet during the composition of the *Comices Agricoles*, as we have seen. He has grafted the Proser-pine legend on to his main theme, just as, when writing *Salammbô*, he will tell Feydeau he is doing with Proserpine and Tanit.[51] Of Emma–Proserpine we have already seen something, and there will be much more to say.

In the meantime, we note how, present at the *Comices*, suggesting a 'dieu caché', is a reminder of the sun-god (all the sun-gods), watching and registering, as a statue of the veiled goddess had already seemed to do at La Vaubyessard, the actions and state of mind of the faltering Emma: 'un grand taureau noir . . . et qui ne bougeait pas plus qu'une bête de bronze.' Sparks seem to Emma to emanate from the eyes of Rodolphe, who has in his first name the wolf of the sun, for he is a composite character like all those in *Madame Bovary*, fusing a series of types. As Charles wears a com-posite 'casquette', so Rodolphe wears heterogeneous clothing. His character at the *Comices* seems moreover to be based directly upon Ovid's advice in *The Art of Love*, not only for his glib, cynical love-making and his belief in a bold approach, but in this assorted garb, the 'négligé' of which he pretends to excuse to Emma. 'Forma viros neglecta decet; Minoida Theseus/Abstulit,' Ovid's words run. The prescription comes directly from the poet's telling of a further mystic marriage, that of Ariadne, sister of Phaedra and Theseus, the solar hero who came across the seas to Crete to abduct her, he whose hair, in Ovid's account, had never known curling-iron or pin, but rose straight from his brow (Emma will later include a similar detail in her mental portrait of Rodolphe). Are we to regard *The Art of Love* simply as one of Flaubert's sources of Rodolphe's technique of seduction, or did he here intend a literary allusion which he assumed some of his readers would recognize? However it may be, Charles, with the three days' beard and dirty fingernails noted by Rodolphe when he first meets him, is, as we might expect, offending against Ovid's recommendations to the successful lover in the same passage. The 'négligé' is assumed; in Charles's case it is plain self-neglect, betokening a tragic lack of sensitivity and even intelligence, in contrast with the perspicacious Rodolphe.

Now Ariadne is another representative soul longing for the godhead. In the ancient mysteries, she is figured in her relations with both Theseus, who deserted her, and with Dionysus–Bacchus, who came to her on Naxos and finally transmuted her into a constellation. Is this not like Emma? We have seen her in Part One in the role of the disconsolate, bereft Isis, cheated, so she feels, of her god. At the same time was she not already at Tostes 'Ariane aux rochers contant ses injustices'—crying aloud to the ruins of Banneville: 'Pourquoi, mon Dieu! me suis-je mariée?' At this point, is not Charles (who had 'saved' her father, as Theseus had Minos) a failed Theseus in her life, as he is an unrecognized Eros, an inadequate Hephaestus, and a ravished Osiris? Afterwards, when she has travelled to La Vaubyessard where the *vicomte* introduces her to champagne and a new, whirling dance, only to forget her, Flaubert shows her scanning the horizon for some sign of a sail, again an Ariadne, abandoned by a false Dionysus: 'Comme les matelots en détresse, elle promenait sur la solitude de sa vie des yeux désespérés, cherchant au loin quelque voile blanche dans les brumes de l'horizon.' To escape from Tostes is now her determination, hubristically convinced as she is that life elsewhere must provide an improvement. Alas for Emma, neither her character nor that of Charles has changed with their geographical circumstances. The 'type' situations which Flaubert invented for them at Tostes will be reenacted at Yonville. Returning unsuccoured from her visit to Bournisien, Emma will again be surrounded by water: a room transformed 'en ondulations' and furniture floating in an 'océan ténébreux'. At the *Comices Agricoles*, as Rodolphe calls into his play his seductive verbal skills (there will be more about these later), Emma continues to be presented against a background of seascape, suggested by the very animals whose simultaneous significance we have already seen: 'sur la longue ondulation de tous ces corps tassés on voyait se lever au vent, comme un flot, quelque crinière blanche, ou bien saillir des cornes aiguës.'

When Emma later submits to Rodolphe in the forest, imagery evocative of sea and water again appears, further continuing the suggestion of Ariadne, abandoned on her island, particularly in the evocation of 'des grèves que le vent remuait'. How can we not at the same time be reminded of the Minerva whom Emma had first aspired to resemble and whom she now offends eternally, for the valley below appears as a 'lac pâle' (one of Minerva's names was Tritogenesis, 'born of the lake')? Emma is moreover veiled like the goddess in Isis form, with the result that 'on distinguait son visage dans une transparence bleuâtre', as though, Venus Anadyomene herself, 'elle eût nage sur des flots d'azur'. Thus, woman and all nature are here liquefied into the humidity J.-P. Richard identified with love and that we have also seen Flaubert identify with matter and the female. And Emma, 'en amazone', thus claiming kinship with the chaste Diana, as had Hippolyta, queen of the Amazons, first bride of Theseus, is revealed (despite aspirations to spirituality and mystery) as being in the grip of the Venus whom we have already discerned within her.

Later instances of sea imagery respond ironically, as always in this book, to Emma's confident defiance of the possible anguish which the hoped-for sail might bring into her life, taken even further on her first night at Yonville when she proclaims to Léon her love for the sea. The irony is in line, for instance, with her longing for wheeled vehicles, none of which, when they appear, will be quite what she had desired. Similarly, she had been prepared to accept any arrival from the ocean, provided something came. After the *Comices*, the 'tangage' of the Counsellor's carriage establishes a clear connection between the motions of the sea, *ivresse*, and wheeled vehicles. The coachman is literally drunk; Homais complains about it ('on devrait sévir contre l'ivresse'), calling our attention to the theme by stressing it. Emma's longing for the *ivresse* which she associates with love, like that of Ariadne, is, we perceive, about to be granted—ironically, of course. The re-entry of Dionysus, waiting in the offing, in a much more violent form than the *vicomte*'s champagne at La Vaubyessard, is indicated.

The sea will continue to be associated with the turning of wheels, the wheels of ironic fate, as the book proceeds, and Dionysus the shape-shifter will, as I have said earlier, take many forms in Emma's life. In her first episode with Rodolphe, 'l'amour l'avait d'abord enivrée', and, as they made love in the garden, 'd'immenses vagues noires' formed by the hissing shadows of trees already seemed to threaten to overwhelm them. Rodolphe's basic brutality, their reduction of their great love to a tranquil 'flamme domestique', led Emma to repent like Hippolyta her submission to him and her subsequent loss of liberty. We now understand Flaubert's removal from the final text of his earlier references to Hippolytus, son of Theseus and Hippolyta (see Chapter Two). Flaubert needed the name to describe the outcome of Emma's first relationship 'en amazone' with Rodolphe–Theseus, namely Charles's attempt, largely at her instigation, to cure the stable-boy Hippolyte, even as the god Esculapius, patron of doctors and relevant to Charles (see Chapter Three), had once brought back to life the real Hippolytus. The surgeon Canivet arrives in a cabriolet to amputate the young man's leg. His cure is not to be the glory of Yonville after all. Charles is yet another failed god for Emma. The cabriolet tilts, storm-tossed or drunken, as it moves away, taking with it the end of another aspiration in Emma's life, that of being the wife of a great man, another version of marriage to a deity. Now it is Charles, tragically evolving into a different form of Dionysus, the victim, the 'son of the wine-cask', as Aristophanes describes him in *The Frogs*, who has 'le regard trouble d'un homme ivre' and who feels about him 'quelque chose de funeste et d'incompréhensible', while his imagination 'ballottait . . . comme un tonneau vide emporté à la mer et qui roule sur les flots'. Emma's desires and dreams for herself have redounded upon her, as has her bravado in the face of possible mishaps.

After the resumption of her affair with Rodolphe, she becomes reduced to 'une sorte d'attachement idiot plein d'admiration pour lui, de voluptés pour elle, une béatitude qui l'engourdissait; et son âme s'enfonçait en cette ivresse et s'y noyait, ratatinée, comme le duc de Clarence dans son tonneau de malvoisie'. Herself the victim now of a debasing, degrading Bacchus, metamorphosed into 'quelque chose de souple et de corrompu', a maenad in the making, her solution to ordinary living is again *flight*, a desire to be 'enlevée', to lead an existence between heaven and earth such as she describes to Rodolphe: 'ce sera comme si nous montions en ballon, comme si nous partions vers les nuages'. 'Haletante, éperdue, ivre' (an aspect of the Dionysiac theme, filled as it is with foreboding, is that Flaubert's characters can be intoxicated with pain and sorrow as well as with alcohol), she will be forced to take refuge in the upper storey of her house in order to read in private the letter which Rodolphe sends, shattering all her hopes. Her own particular bark is now a prey to violence and the floor of the attic where she stands seems to her to slope 'à la manière d'un vaisseau qui tangue', the wheels this time being present in the form of Binet's lathe. She falls ill but is never converted to reality, still seeing the only answer as an escape elsewhere, longing, like Ariadne, to become a constellation, a group of those stars Flaubert has shown us glittering above the Norman countryside: 'Elle entrevit, parmi les illusions de son espoir, un état de pureté flottant au-dessus de la terre, se confondant avec le ciel et où elle aspira d'être.' All that remains with her of the experience is 'le sentiment vague d'une immense duperie'—the great danger of excessive aspirations, as Flaubert knew and showed so well.

Part Three of the novel continues to show Emma against a background of seascape, still frequently associated with the progress of wheels. At the opera, the singing seems to her to be 'des cris de naufragés dans le tumulte d'une tempête', the cab in which she submits to Léon is 'ballottée comme un navire', the old diligence descending into Rouen 'se balançait', surrounded by 'coups de vent' that resemble 'des flots aériens'. The result of it all will again be an Emma–Ariadne 'furetant d'un œil en pleurs l'horizon vide'. She will long again to escape, alone this time, into 'les espaces immaculés', recalling the wish of a more recent Psyche–Ariadne–Venus, the *Jeune Parque* of Valéry:

> Que dans le ciel placés, mes yeux tracent mon temple!
> Et que sur moi repose un autel sans exemple![52]

when the burden of existence and its implications have become clear and unbearable to her also. But the 'Jeune Parque', unlike Emma, rejects self-destruction and ends by accepting the god who comes out of the sea, in spite of herself, that is, in full knowledge of the rebarbative as well as the glorious elements her submission implies. Emma believes she knows that what comes out of the sea, shining in radiance though they may at first be, are not gods but men. She dies even more to escape from Charles and the intolerable weight of his magnanimity than from Léon's cowardice, Guillaumin's lechery,

Binet's shocked disapproval, the disappointment of her whole relationship with Rodolphe, and from Lheureux and existence itself. 'Tout suicide est peut-être un assassinat rentré,'[53] Flaubert wrote in the correspondence. We think of Lucie de Lammermoor, with whom Emma had identified herself at the opera, and who did indeed kill her unwanted husband. Charles will die just as surely.

One of the most celebrated sentences in *Madame Bovary* concerns Emma's disillusionment as her relationship with Léon deteriorates: 'Elle avait trouvé dans l'adultère toutes les platitudes du mariage.' For indeed, as part of the major metaphor at the heart of *Madame Bovary,* each of Emma's relationships is specifically referred to in terms of a marriage. Thus, already at the end of her first relationship with Rodolphe, 'quand le printemps arriva, ils se trouvaient, l'un vis-à-vis de l'autre, comme deux mariés qui entretenaient tranquillement une flamme domestique'. And in Part Three, Emma's life and experience will, as we have seen, start again and follow the same progression as in both other parts but with ever more violence and speed, culminating in a headlong descent into tragedy.

In the final stages of her second (Dionysiac) episode with Rodolphe, it had seemed clear that Emma–Psyche had left behind her all traces of Athene. When she walked with Rodolphe smoking a cigarette 'comme pour narguer le monde', or when she was seen stepping from the *Hirondelle* wearing a waistcoat like a man's (or that of the young George Sand), the androgyne she evoked was no longer Pallas but the hermaphrodite literally issued from the union between Hermes (it is not difficult to see that the god of travel and harbinger of death is another element in the composite Rodolphe) and Aphrodite, the 'Vénus impudique' who had assumed power over Emma. Yet, after the illness brought on by Rodolphe's desertion, a desire to become pure spirit came once more upon Emma in her religious phase; again the church (as formerly Bournisien alone) failed her, this time in its literature and in its ignorance and indifference to the needs of 'une personne du sexe qui a beaucoup d'esprit'. It is to the theatre, temple of Dionysus himself, prompted not only by Homais the busybody but also, ironically, by Bournisien, music being in his eyes less dangerous than literature, that Charles takes Emma to complete her convalescence. In both early versions of *Saint Antoine,* Dionysus is addressed as 'Père des théâtres';[54] Ovid's *Art of Love* recommends the theatre as unfailingly propitious to love-affairs. The opera in question, *Lucie de lammermoor,*

Flaubert had recently seen at Constantinople; its story (there is a French as well as an Italian version of Donizetti's work) was calculated to call upon the literary memories of Emma, avid reader of Walter Scott, while impressing upon her its similarity with elements in her own life, thus taking her right back to the beginning, annulling the lessons she might have learned, even providing in the person of the singer Lagardy, with his hackneyed Don Juan Tenorio attributes, another divinity and object of longing. The transition to Léon is admirable.

Emma's illusions about herself are not dead as she sits facing Léon, with 'comme un fond d'or derrière elle'—the yellow ('safran') hangings of the hotel room, colour of the wallpaper of Tostes where she had begun her married life, colour of her gown at another initiatory ceremony, the ball at La Vaubyessard, colour of the dress she wore when first she met Rodolphe, colour of the curtains in his bedroom at La Huchette, colour (significantly) of the dawn and of 'flavia Minerva'. At the theatre, so we learn through Léon's thoughts, Emma had worn the *lorgnon* of our first sight of her. But Flaubert's words 'une exquise candeur s'échappait de son maintien' do not now apply to Emma but to the young man before her. His timidity is 'plus dangereuse pour elle que la hardiesse de Rodolphe quand il s'avançait les bras ouverts. Jamais aucun homme ne lui avait paru si beau.' For taking Mars as a lover, the saffron-robed dawn-maiden Eos was cursed by Aphrodite with a constant longing for young mortals. After her adultery with the brutal Rodolphe, Flaubert now proceeds to show us Emma passing through metamorphoses of similar 'types' in fiction and mythology, still craving for the godhead but now in the form of younger heroes, all integrated into the overall pattern of the book as we have been able to discern it. She resists Léon temporarily and sends him away, making an appointment with him at the cathedral (like a 'dame andalouse' going to meet her Don Juan–Lagardy of the previous evening). There, still seeking to escape Léon, 'elle se raccrochait de sa vertu chancelante à la Vierge, aux sculptures, aux tombeaux, à toutes les occasions', all turning into blasphemy and offence when a *fiacre* and the habits of Paris quickly conquer an Emma who had for so long desired to be rushed away in a wheeled vehicle by an importunate lover. The outcome is a relationship in which the dominant role is hers.

From virginal *candeur* and an aspiration to be spirit and intelligence, Emma–Psyche has now evolved by way of disillusion and sexual adventures to the role of willingly and hopefully fostering that 'culte de la mère' which Flaubert found so significant for his own age. To what does she now aspire? Which mystic marriages will she now reenact?

One mythical and literary relationship between a mother and her son leaps immediately to mind, that of Phaedra and Hippolytus or, in a French context, Racine's Phèdre and Hippolyte. The young solar hero had already been mentioned in the rough drafts of early chapters; his name had been given to the outcome of Emma's first union 'en amazone' with Rodolphe; Phèdre's sister Ariane is an important contributory figure in both earlier parts of the book and has been shown to be significantly present in Part Three.

CHAPTER FIVE

'Weaving spiders, come not here'

> Il faut, dans la traduction des œuvres d'art philosophiques, apporter une grande minutie et une grande attention; là, les lieux, le décor, les meubles, les ustensiles . . . , tout est allégorie, allusion, hiéroglyphes, rébus.[1]

'Je n'ai pas dansé, pourtant, je n'ai pas aimé, je n'ai pas bu,' laments the expiring Minerva in the first version of *Saint Antoine*.[2] The version of 1856 retains almost the same words. Emma likewise in Flaubert's rough drafts had never drunk alcohol.[3] In the definitive text she will drink a very little curaçao in a scene where her delicate sipping of the liquid evokes a bee, like the *papillon* an ancient symbol of the human soul. Curaçao is made from the orange, an attribute of Bacchus, according to the 1849 *Saint Antoine*,[4] as well as being associated with marriages, as the two wedding bouquets of orange blossom which occur in *Madame Bovary* remind us. One thinks too of Flaubert's complaint about women who ask for oranges from apple trees,[5] a category to which the Norman country girl Emma might well be said to belong. The scene provides Emma with an opportunity to invite Charles to drink with her, a custom signifying a convocation to rather more in ancient Gaul and which the innocent Salammbô will also unwittingly follow. 'A quand les noces?' a mercenary asks Mâtho.[6] Flaubert had already taken note of a similar superstition in North Africa during the Eastern voyage, and of course the love philtres of the ancient as well as the medieval world come to mind. Clearly, for Flaubert Emma was here performing—albeit unknowingly—a time-honoured rite. And it is she who—Eve and eternal feminine—takes the initiative.

Alcohol is naturally an important aspect of the theme of *ivresse*, literal and figurative, in *Madame Bovary*. At La Vaubyessard, Emma notices that 'plusieurs dames n'avaient pas mis leurs gants dans leur verre', that is to say, that they were intending to drink wine with their meal. Emma, we assume, follows their example, since we see her initiated into the *frissons* imparted by champagne, a luxury which by the end of the book she will require as essential in her meetings with Léon, accompanying its consumption with a 'rire sonore et libertin'. This is the symmetry we have grown to expect in *Madame Bovary*, just as the ice she savours, eyes closed, at La Vaubyessard (we note the colour and form of its receptacle—'une coquille de vermeil') is re-echoed on several occasions: Charles sipping one 'à petits coups' outside the theatre, Emma and Léon ordering 'sorbets à la glace' to be sent up to their bedroom 'dès le matin', Charles and Justin ironically unable to obtain ice for Emma on her deathbed. Thus, throughout the novel, the advancing cold of winter on the one hand and of the inevitable tomb on the other is heralded and emphasized.

Minerva had not danced, but dancing is an art Emma has learned at her more modern academy for young ladies. The significantly circular waltz is yet new to her, and her initiation into it by the *vicomte* is balanced when the dizziness it caused is reproduced as she is almost run down by a vehicle she believes him to be driving on the last day of her life. 'Elle se sentait perdue, roulant au hasard dans des abîmes indéfinissables.' At the bacchic masked ball where she performs a less refined dance—'elle sauta toute la nuit au son des trombones'—it is she who is now the centre of a circle of admirers as at La Vaubyessard the expert in waltzing had been. By the light of day, how great does she see her social descent to have been! In one rough draft, Flaubert summed up the effect of La Vaubyessard upon Emma as resembling that of a drop of red wine in a glass of water. No doubt he perceived that here, as in other cases, the themes of both *ivresse* and the colour red were too obvious too soon. The reference he retained instead combines the recurrent theme of feet and footwear as representing the material and the earthbound with the colour yellow. The sole of each dancing shoe 's'était jaunie à la cire glissante du parquet. Son cœur était comme eux.' The candid androgyne has become overtly female; the pure white dawn has grown yellow, as her wedding-dress had been exchanged for a yellow ball-gown.

There is more to the presence of Minerva in *Madame Bovary* than this particular depiction of Emma's decline. In an early scenario she had been seen 'près de sa lampe et de ses broderies'. The lamp, like her *candeur*, I have associated with Psyche; the 'broderies', like the bold eyes, evoke Minerva–Ergana. Indeed, Emma from an early stage had been intended to excel at 'les choses de la main', and although in keeping with her general development she gradually tosses aside these activities as unsatisfying, the references to sewing, darning, embroidery, spinning, and weaving do, when considered together in the form of a series of related allusions, form a consistent framework comprehensible on both a literal and a figurative level.

Thus, in our (and Charles's) first encounter with Emma, plain sewing is shown to be neither her habit nor her interest. To begin with, she cannot find her needle-case; when she does start sewing the 'coussins' for her father's splints, she repeatedly pricks her fingers. Throughout the book her husband's shirts and her daughter's stockings will usually lack buttons and exhibit holes 'au grand scandale de Madame Homais'. In a memorable scene with Charles (which we shall have occasion to discuss later) it is true that he finds her in the semi-darkness engaged in the humble task of darning a white stocking; later, when Léon unexpectedly calls on her in Yonville, she snatches up a towel and—again the perfect housewife— is modestly drawing a grey thread through it when he comes into the room. But the role she chooses for herself is usually in a less humdrum category. During Emma's religious phase, when saintly humility is her aim, her mother-in-law cannot forbear feeling irritated by Emma's mania for knitting camisoles for orphans 'au lieu de raccommoder les torchons'. And the related activity which Emma has learnt at her convent, together with music and geography, is one in which she does at first show considerable interest. Having received 'une belle éducation', Mademoiselle Rouault 'sait faire de la tapisserie'. When she marries Charles, her ability to embroider slippers for him will be not the least cause of his pride in her, and it will be one of the accomplishments he dreams of his daughter also possessing. Embroidery, like all forms of needlework, is a theme in the book which is specifically connected with Emma. Images referring to tapestry work are attributed by Flaubert to Emma's dream of a woman's life, as, again and again after the ball at La Vaubyessard, she gazes at the embroidered cigar case with its inscription 'Amor nel Cor': 'Un souffle d'amour avait passé parmi les mailles du canevas; chaque coup d'aiguille avait fixé là une espérance ou un souvenir, et tous ces fils de soie entrelacés n'étaient que la continuité de la même passion silencieuse.' Later, we see Emma, herself in mute love with Léon after her arrival at Yonville, moving over to the window each morning, waiting for the sight of Léon passing by on his way to his office. At night, when the second of the day's great moments for her comes about—Léon's return past the window to his lodgings—her hands, we are told, are idle in her lap, her needlework neglected. Embroidery, like her later efforts to improve her mind with instructional reading, becomes something embarked on enthusiastically with a kind of hope of salvation, only to be left unfinished, replaced by some new panacea: 'il en était de ses lectures comme de ses tapisseries, qui, toutes commencées, encombraient son armoire; elle les prenait, les quittait, passait à d'autres.' But if embroidery, taken as the literal embellishment of plain fabric, is abandoned by Emma, she becomes progressively more accomplished at the figurative embellishment of plain truth. The girl who at confession had already fabricated small sins to make herself interesting complains to Rodolphe about Charles, 'exagérant les faits, en inventant plusieurs', then goes on later to talk to Léon of a sea-captain admirer in order to increase her prestige with him. Finally, with regard to her visits to Rouen, she becomes addicted to lying to Charles: 'A partir de ce moment, son existence ne fut plus qu'un assemblage de mensonges, où elle enveloppait son amour comme dans des voiles, pour le cacher. C'était un besoin, une manie, un plaisir.' We realize, moreover, that the two notions, accomplishment with needle and with words, had been associated by Flaubert from the beginning. Emma, in the view of Charles's jealous first wife, had been 'quelqu'un qui savait causer, une brodeuse'.

Emma had woven a fabric of lies in order to conceal from Charles her affair with Léon 'comme dans des voiles'. The expression here reminds us less of embroidery than of the associated skills of spinning and weaving, and in particular of the references to spiders and their webs with which Flaubert intersperses his narrative: 'On pourrait presque parler d'un thème de l'araignée dans *Madame Bovary*,' says Bopp,[7] and this we shall look at in more detail later. First, in order to state our main argument, let us recall that, as her sensual appetites grow, the luxurious products of other people's spinning and weaving—'des rideaux à larges raies jaunes', a carpet beneath her feet—are part of Emma's resort for comfort and consolation, and that a social fact—namely how, in the community in which she lived, linen-weaving was becoming an important industry—is stressed by Flaubert. At the *Comices Agricoles* great emphasis is twice laid by the counsellor on the increasing significance, as a local crop, of *le lin*. On neither occasion is Emma listening. Homais had already also pompously discoursed on the marvels to be performed in a half-completed linen factory which, before Léon's departure, the two families had visited in his company. Emma's unspoken reaction—'Rien, pourtant, n'était moins curieux que cette curiosité'—is exactly in line with her later lack of interest in the 'scène de la folie' at the Opera, for just as she herself will be fated to play out her own scene of madness and suicide, so will the lot of her daughter Berthe, around whom so many dreams had once been spun—before her birth by Emma and afterwards by Charles—be that of child-labour in one of these very 'filatures'. Flaubert takes the point one step further: the child will be a spinner neither of exotic silk nor of home-grown flax, but of cotton, a reminder of all that this purported for the development of nineteenth-century industrial society.

Emma's hubristic presumption, her aspirations and incurable pretensions, all these, combined with the themes I have mentioned, lead us to the conclusion that, as Richard B. Grant once suggested in a short note,[8] we have here as substructure of Flaubert's novel one of the best-known myths concerning the goddess Minerva, namely, the story of Arachne. Arachne, a maid of humble origin, having presumed to challenge Minerva herself to a contest in the art of weaving, was punished by the jealous goddess with such severe blows to the head that the girl hanged herself. Minerva, relenting, turned her into a spider and decreed that all her progeny after her should spend their lives spinning out webs, as spiders too.

Flaubert's book does not end with the death of Emma. From the moment she dies, her influence, as is well known, reaches out to Charles: 'Elle le corrompait par delà le tombeau.' Like her, he becomes at first a spinner of romantic dreams, then disillusioned and betrayed in his worship of her, yet dying, as she had, still unwilling to surrender the picture he had set before him, holding, significantly, a lock of her silky hair in his hands. Other people who had felt Emma's influence are comparable. Félicité, the servant, trained by Emma, sharing all her mistress's secrets, yet learning nothing from her vile death, eventually runs off with her lover as Emma had desired to do. The fact that there is one character, Justin, whom in Emma's presence we had seen 'debout, les mains pendantes, les yeux ouverts, comme enlacé dans les fils innombrables d'une rêverie soudaine', but who breaks through the web and escapes, only to become a grocer's assistant, augments the poignant complexity of the author's theme. The fate of a literal 'spinner' reserved for Berthe, Emma's actual daughter, is one of the brutal truths which explain the book's extraordinary power. Seen as the culmination of a carefully designed pattern of imagery, its tragic impact is, I suggest, intensified.

All this is reason enough for our at least agreeing with Grant in postulating the existence of the Arachne myth in the background of the story of the presumptuous Emma, who also takes her own life, and in whose eyes, as she lies dead, it seems to Charles that spiders have woven their webs: 'ses yeux commençaient à disparaître dans une pâleur visqueuse qui ressemblait à une toile mince, comme si les araignées avaient filé dessus.' When we look at the story of Arachne in more detail, further points occur to us. Arachne's tapestry, in which Minerva could find no fault, and which therefore inspired her to fury and revenge, had incorporated representations of the deceitful loves of the gods. Here a number of factors arise. The imagery we have noted in *Madame Bovary* seems to suggest that the web which Emma is attempting to spin, embellish, enshroud in mystery, is in fact that of her own life. At the same time, as though to underline her presumption in making such an attempt, the continual hum of Binet's lathe in the background, especially at certain important points in the book—such as when she is reading Rodolphe's treacherous letter or on the last day of her life—is made to suggest the whirring of the wheel of the Fates themselves, endlessly at work as the Greeks conceived them to be. In the same category as the lathe are all the wheeled vehicles which Flaubert has been called self-indulgent for describing with such care, all of which are connected with cardinal incidents in Emma's life—her wedding, the ball at La Vaubyessard, the move to Yonville, the *Hirondelle* with its trail of dust, Rodolphe running away and leaving her behind, the *fiacre*, the tilbury in which she imagines from time to time that she sees the *vicomte*, wheels turning endlessly, never quite those that Emma had dreamed of, yet for many of which she cannot disclaim responsibility. A scene in which she herself is shown turning a kind of wheel is provided by Flaubert's description of a social evening *chez les Homais*, when Emma listens to Léon reading to her from the Romantic poets, 'en faisant tourner machinalement l'abat-jour de la lampe'. Even the subjects painted upon the lampshade have relevance to our theme: 'des pierrots dans des voitures et des danseuses de corde, avec leurs balanciers'.

Here we pause to think of Emma's name before marriage. Although originally, as we know from Flaubert's notes, his heroine's

name was to have been Lestiboudois, the metaphors which sprang
unbidden to his mind seem to have been heeded by him sufficiently
for him to adopt, instead, the name Rouault. That Flaubert's names
are symbolic we have already seen, and once this is accepted,it is not
difficult to perceive a symbolic association between Emma *Rouault*
and the legendary Arachne, always remembering that Minerva is
goddess of both spinning and weaving and that both go together in
Flaubert's synthesis of images. The name of Berthe's foster-mother,
la mère Rolet, who nursed the child though her true mother had
changed her name to Bovary, adds depth to the device, especially
since, when Emma visits la mère Rolet on the afternoon before her
suicide, throwing herself upon a bed and staring up at a spider
crawling across the ceiling, we are told that 'la bonne femme
s'éloigna, prit son rouet et se mit à filer du lin'. La mère Rolet acts as
intermediary in Emma's affair with Léon, and when Emma lies on
her deathbed it will be Berthe's mention of *nourrice* that conjures up
for her the spectacle of the life which, abetted by all the intangibles
that go to make up an existence she herself had fabricated, 'ce nom,
qui la reportait dans le souvenir de ses adultères et de ses calamités'.

By the end of her life, the web of existence which Emma had
woven for herself does indeed, like the web of Arachne, seem to her
the history of a series of disillusions and betrayed dreams. If she is an
Arachne figure, we need also to be aware in the book of two things
more: in the first place of instances in which Emma, a modern
Arachne, is seen to be vying with the goddess as in the ancient
legend; secondly, of episodes or images suggesting that revenge, as
also in the legend, is being sought, meditated, prepared for her, by
the goddess on this account.

It is in the scenes concerning spiders that Flaubert shows us
clearly how Emma, Arachne-like, is setting herself up in rivalry to
the goddess, that is, presumptuously assuming her capacity to com-
pose the pattern of her own life. There is the episode, already briefly
referred to, when Charles, at three o'clock on a hot afternoon, finds
Emma darning in a shuttered kitchen: 'Par les fentes de bois, le soleil
allongeait sur les pavés de grandes raies minces, qui se brisaient à
l'angle des meubles et tremblaient au plafond.' In the darkness of this
most suggestive web 'Charles n'aperçut pas d'abord Emma'. His
position is emphasized for us by the presence in the room of insects:
'Des mouches, sur la table, montaient le long des verres qui avaient
servi et bourdonnaient en se noyant au fond, dans le cidre resté' (the

modest stocking-mender has not yet cleared the table after the midday meal). We know little of Emma as yet, but suspect she has laid a trap for the young doctor whom her father esteems as 'un homme de grande capacité' (our suspicions are confirmed later by her behaviour with the young Léon); the buzzing of the flies is echoed when, as Charles thinks of Emma, 'quelque chose de monotone comme le ronflement d'une toupie bourdonnait à ses oreilles: "Si tu te mariais, pourtant, si tu te mariais!"' He is caught for ever in her meshes, victim of an enchantress whose turn, however, is soon to come, for the goddess, as the ancients knew, is merciless. The result is a marriage in which Emma finds herself victim: 'Mais, elle, sa vie était froide, comme un grenier dont la lucarne est au nord, et l'ennui, araignée silencieuse, filait sa toile dans l'ombre, à tous les coins de son cœur.' As for the flies, she will find herself in their position also, sodden with sweetness like the Duke of Clarence in his butt of malmsey, a simile almost invariably criticized adversely, yet, in the light of our theme, revealed as part of the unity of the book's structural imagery.

A further relevant scene describing an insect occurs at an early stage in Emma's relationship with Léon. The young man and woman are returning together along the river bank after paying a visit, significantly, to the house of la mère Rolet. Like their life and their love at this time, the stream is limpid, the air calm: 'Quelquefois, à la pointe des joncs ou sur la feuille des nénufars, un insecte à pattes fines marchait ou se posait.' We do not know if the 'insects' are spiders or their possible victims, whether to identify them with Emma or with Léon or with the goddess spinning her web unheeded in the background, and we savour the ambiguity which, alerted as we have been by the webbed kitchen and the 'araignée silencieuse', suggests to us the possible ironies which fate may hold in store for both these young people, walking now in the sunshine.

In what other ways does Flaubert show that, somewhere in the offing, a power, aware of Emma's presumption, is determined to punish it? As the book proceeds, we are conscious of an accumulation of vengeance, woven into the texture of the novel. To select a very few examples, when Emma submits to Rodolphe, the 'cri doux et rauque' of Minerva's crows can be heard in the forest; Emma will hear them again during her mad rush home through the gathering darkness after her last disappointment with Rodolphe: 'La nuit tombait; les corneilles volaient.' Poised before the attic window, reading Rodolphe's deceitful letter, she hears in Binet's lathe a 'voix furieuse' calling her to throw herself down; she will imagine she hears the lathe again in the hum of the nurse's spinning-wheel on the final afternoon of her life. As she stands in the *ruelle* with Léon, the sky rumbles thunderously and lightning flashes in the distance. So, in her youth, had she imagined the onset of love; now, as she accepts love for the third time, we sense that the last act of Emma's tragedy has begun. Yet there is in Flaubert no suggestion of melodrama, only of the pity and relentlessness of it all. On the last night of her life, as the distraught woman rushes downhill to her death, dry leaves beneath the feet which had once formed a bed for lovers have changed into an obstacle. Already, as she had left the Guillaumin house, 'il lui semblait que la Providence s'acharnait à la poursuivre'.

Moreover, although Emma, unlike Arachne, does not hang herself, yet how ironic had been her dream of an ideal existence glimpsed at the château of La Vaubyessard: 'C'était une existence au-dessus des autres, entre ciel et terre, dans les nuages, quelque chose de sublime.' More than once, too, she sees yawning before her a terri-fying gulf, *l'abîme*. Just as Minerva strikes Arachne on the head with the shuttle of her loom, so Emma, who, when she first met Rodolphe, could claim (though inaccurately) that she never in her life fainted, receives metaphorical blows of such force that on each occasion she falls senseless—or nearly so. When Emma made her claim to Rodolphe, she had forgotten the birth of her daughter—a daughter for Emma, who had aspired to be the mother of a man: '"C'est une fille," dit Charles. Elle tourna la tête et s'évanouit.' She fainted again after receiving Rodolphe's letter, once more following the realization of the nature of the masked ball she had attended, as a result of her treatment at the hands of Lheureux: 'Elle s'affaissa, plus assommée qu'elle n'eût été par un coup de massue,' and when, in the streets of Rouen, she is almost knocked down by a tilbury, she imagines for a moment that its passenger was the *vicomte*, who had danced with her long ago at the ball at La Vaubyessard: 'Au reste, elle n'en savait rien. Tout, en elle-même et au dehors, l'abandonnait. Elle se sentait perdue, roulant au hasard dans des abîmes indéfinissables.' Finally, after Rodolphe's refusal of help:

La folie la prenait, elle eut peur et parvint à se ressaisir, d'une manière confuse, il est vrai; car elle ne se rappelait point la cause de son horrible état, c'est-à-dire la question d'argent. Elle ne souffrait que de son amour . . . Alors sa situation, telle qu'un abîme, se présenta. Elle haletait à se rompre la poitrine.

Then, in a 'transport d'héroïsme', she ran down the hill to the chemist's shop to procure the poison. In Ovid's telling of the tale, Hecate's herbs had been sprinkled by Minerva upon the hanging body of the presumptuous spinner. Flaubert's modern Arachne, such is the balance in the book between personal responsibility and those external factors the Greeks called destiny, finds the poison and inflicts it upon herself. Her actual death might yet well be a description of strangulation: 'Sa poitrine se mit aussitôt à haleter rapidement. La langue tout entière lui sortit hors de la bouche ... ses côtes, secouées par un souffle furieux, comme si l'âme eût fait des bonds pour se détacher.'

So detailed a study of one of the patterns of imagery wherewith Flaubert expresses 'le dessous' of his work can be completed more briefly by other elements indicating the presence of Minerva. Thus triangles formed by scarves, shawls, and handkerchiefs, pyramids by fruit; lampions decorating La Vaubyessard and the *Comices* (in the rough drafts, supported by the correspondence, there was to have been much more emphasis on them[9]); the moon, rising first purple and then turning to dazzling white, shedding light upon the river to form at the same time a snake and a candelabra; the many *flambeaux* which we see Emma lighting or in her neighbourhood; all these are attributes of Athene–Minerva, the 'déesse cachée sous le tissu cosmique', in the words of Guignault's translation of Creuzer.

Then there are further webs formed by the light on the portraits at La Vaubyessard and by the sun on the stones of the cathedral in Rouen, and the web of a darn which Emma stares at in her table napkin after reading Rodolphe's letter. But as well as Arachne, Emma reproduces another victim of Minerva's resentment, Iodamie, who also set herself up as a false Minerva and who one night was turned to stone in the temple by the sight of the Gorgon's head upon the breast of the real goddess. So Emma, when she turns away from Bournisien and the church, swivels round 'tout d'un bloc comme une statue sur un pivot'. Like Iodamie, she had longed for light and has glimpsed darkness and shadows (the sense of the Gorgon's head). 'La matière l'emporta sur l'esprit, l'obscurité sur la lumière ... elle ne put vaincre le ténébreux égarement qui s'empara de ses sens,' runs Creuzer's description of Iodamie. The resemblance to Flaubert's description of Emma's subsequent state of mind is striking, as was the case with the words quoted earlier from Creuzer's account of the Psyche myth. 'Le lendemain fut, pour Emma, une journée funèbre,'

he writes of the day following Léon's departure. 'Tout lui parut
enveloppé par une atmosphère noire qui flottait confusément sur
l'extérieur des choses.' We see that part of the value that Emma's
mythical counterparts have for Flaubert is that her metamorphoses
are instruments of psychological analysis. If Flaubert follows
Creuzer and Ovid so closely, it is because they provide him with
variants upon the relationship within the consciousness of spirit and
matter and also at the same time with imagery to express them. 'Nous
sommes trop avancés en fait d'art pour nous tromper sur la nature,'
he had written to Bouilhet from Egypt,[10] and in this he surely
included human nature. Can we not postulate also that when he
spoke of *Madame Bovary* as containing all his 'science psycho-
logique'[11] Flaubert had in mind—at least partly—this technique of
deliberately (as well as unconsciously as happens to all creative
writers) superimposing one upon another 'types' and the images that
express them? Once one has reached a certain stage, he also
declared, 'on ne se trompe plus quant à tout ce qui est de l'âme'.[12] The
'control' is there in the succession of examples which, throughout
history, have seemed significant to artists and to their public.

Aspects of the goddess Minerva can be connected with other
major incidents in Emma's life and may thus have inspired Flaubert
to invent them. At the time of the *pied bot* operation, it is Minerva–
Medica, support and inspiration of the doctor Esculapius, that
Emma is reproducing. When she then reproaches herself for her
mistaken belief in Charles—'elle qui était si intelligente!'—she is
hubristically claiming for herself the characteristic trait of the
goddess. In her musical life, Emma offends Minerva–Musica. In her
financial transactions, her complete lack of *prévoyance* must defy
and give offence. On her last night with Léon in Rouen, her
blasphemy is complete as she dances at the masked ball, a 'lampion
sur l'oreille'. The date, moreover, is the *mi-carême* which in 1846,
apparently the year of Emma's death, fell on 19 March, the day of
Minerva's own feast. As Emma hurries home from the Guillaumin
house, her *orgueil* reasserts itself, for Minerva is the goddess of
persistence in combat. Yet it seems to her that, as we have seen,
Providence was pursuing her: Minerva herself, so Creuzer tells us,
was called the 'providence' of Jupiter.

We have seen in Chapter Two how her early manifestations
involved another goddess of medicine and of the sacrosanct nature
of marriage and of the family, the Egyptian Isis, who was originally a

counterpart of Minerva at Sais in North Africa. Attributes which they have in common recur significantly throughout the book. There is her veil (also associated with Juno in *Saint Antoine* and with Ceres–Proserpine in Creuzer) that figures in Rodolphe's seduction scene and as Emma descends from Léon's *fiacre*. There is the *Hirondelle*, name of the yellow coach which brings the Bovary family to Yonville, which is glimpsed by Emma as she talks to Rodolphe at the *Comices*, which will be used by Emma to carry her to her Thursday assignations with Léon, and which has as its driver Hivert, homonym of Isis' own season and who, like Minerva *memor*, never forgets and finally erupts clattering into Yonville just after Emma's death. Swallows figure in a series of other notations—in the village of Charles's childhood, in Bournisien's church, in relation to Emma's dreams which are like 'hirondelles blessées'. The association becomes more sinister when the weather-vane of Rodolphe's château has a 'queue d'aronde' as Emma hurries to her lover in the early morning. Weather-vanes also figure in the scene where Emma almost throws herself to her death. The wheel motif is in both cases implicit, together with the fact that for Apuleius, as we have seen, Isis was mistress of the elements as of all nature, giving greater significance to the interesting introduction of a barometer into the narrative, to be shaken blasphemously from the wall and smashed by Emma in her anger after the *pied bot* failure. Isis as cat is also present intermittently. In the early drafts, Flaubert had shown Emma attempting to draw a cat sleeping in the sun and succeeding only in delineating one which was running away 'à toutes jambes',[13] this at the period in her life when we have already identified her as Isis in her walks with Djali–Anubis. In the passage which seems to herald Baudelaire's 1862 *Spleen* poem and in which the misery of succeeding weeks is evoked, we are told that 'quelque chat sur les toits, marchant lentement, bombait son dos aux rayons pâles du soleil'. Later, in Rouen, the *chatteries* with which Emma entertains her lover Léon are in blasphemous contrast with those which the devoted mother, Madame Bovary *mère*, had lavished on the infant Charles, and provide another example of the mother–son relationship which we have already seen Emma to have adopted towards the young man. The mythical identities are Isis and the malformed Harpocrates, the feeble winter solstice, whom we see her mourn in *Saint Antoine*, as the virgin mother of Jesus is later to mourn her own son, eventually identified by the Church with the symbolic birth of the new sun also.

In her final scene with Rodolphe, whose past actions Flaubert attributes in so many words to 'cette lâcheté naturelle qui caractérise le sexe fort', Emma ingratiates herself with him 'avec des gestes mignons de tête, plus câline qu'une chatte amoureuse'. Thus again are we reminded of her development from *candeur* by way of false *pudeur* to unbridled sensuality. Something of what happened to the cult of Isis, 'déesse à la fois antérieure et postérieure', between the austere antiquity of Egypt and the reintroduction of Isis–Cybele into imperial Rome is also reflected here, paralleled by the gradual metamorphosis we have noted of Minerva into Venus 'au sourire impudique'. Isis is visible behind all the goddesses. All are, in fact, as Apuleius taught Flaubert, aspects of Isis.

And throughout the book, sinister and persistent, a metallic tinkle is heard, associated at first with Charles's memory of *tringles* on hospital beds as he rides, guided by the moon, towards his first sight of Emma. There are *tringles* among the family effects transported to the new house at Yonville. The sick-bed on which she will die is clearly already implicit. The *grelots* on the horses drawing the *Hirondelle* are mentioned at the same time as the first mention of the blind beggar. The cracked sound of the church bells at Tostes punctuates Emma's melancholy revery there, just as the ringing of the Angelus bell at Yonville will attract her to her abortive attempt to seek solace from Bournisien. The bell of the inn at Tostes also tinkles, as do Homais's scales. Alongside these tinkling noises, there is also rattling—of the metal rings on the firearms of the militiamen at the *Comices*, of the forks of the Homais family, eating away happily as Emma comes to take the arsenic, of the hooves of the *Hirondelle*'s horses, of chairs being shuffled by the crowd at the *Comices*. Most of all, there is the repeated tapping of the blind beggar's stick, which will eventually, along with the sound of his thick 'sabots', signal his arrival at the moment of Emma's death. All these instances culminate in the rattle of the pebbles cast on to Emma's coffin, which fall with 'ce bruit formidable qui nous semble être le retentissement de l'éternité'. Both tinkling and rattling evoke Apuleius' universal mother, mistress of life but also of death, and regularly formed part of the ceremonies in honour of Isis, as Flaubert would know. Perhaps at no moment in the book is the presence of Isis in Emma's background and actuality more stressed than when, in despair, she turns away from Bournisien and his catechism class, hearing behind her the children's reverberating voices—'baptisé . . . , baptisé . . . , baptisé'. In *Bouvard et*

Pécuchet, the Second Empire at an end, Flaubert can be more explicit. In his description of Christianity, Pécuchet will declare in his list of Christian elements found in other religions: 'le baptême était chez Isis.' The water theme, here again in the Church, is then associated in Flaubert's mind with the nature goddess.

One scene in which Emma is clearly impersonating Isis occurs in the boat which carries Emma and Léon back from their island idyll. Tall, black-clad, she appears with the moon behind her head as does Isis in Lucius' vision as recounted by Apuleius. Two heroines who had thus decked themselves out as the goddess were the historical and literary Cleopatra, consciously as Isis herself, and the legendary Psyche, unwittingly as Venus. Salammbô will do likewise in the accoutrement of Tanit. All three are punished. Thus, Flaubert arranges the circumstances of Emma's burial in such a way as to recall the death-boat of Isaic ceremonial. He first contrives an incident in which Emma's coffin is raised to the vertical as in Isaic ritual. We then see the undulating, almost floating progress of her bier towards the cemetery 'comme une chaloupe qui tangue'. And all the water imagery—that which we have associated with Ariadne, with Helen, and with Venus—is shown to be leading to one final moment in Emma's destiny, when, under the guiding hand of the great goddess of nature and therefore of fate, her final journey of return to the earth takes place, that earth from which she came and which she has transcendently represented. Her personal boat has been the vessel which in the deep structure of texts carries a character from birth to death. We see now that it has been specifically for Flaubert the sun-boat of Isis that he saw upon the walls of Egyptian tombs and temples during the journey when his novel was conceived, and as such it has carried Emma from dawn to sunset and from year's beginning to year's end in the old moon-dominated calendar. By the time Emma dies, the candid young girl has herself become 'la mère Bovary' in Flaubert's correspondence, and as in Northern myths the old Queen of the year died in Spring, so does she, in favour of Léon's new fiancée. Flaubert has again set the two visions of Nature, Egyptian and Northern-Celtic, in parallel. The importance of an Isis cult in Gaul was, as we saw, well known to him. The existence of her equivalent, the Gaulish Esus, whose name and being were believed by some commentators to have become amalgamated with her, was also attested by some of his sources.

We have seen how Apuleius taught Flaubert to see Isis as

containing within her all the other great goddesses. Although Creuzer, so far as I can find, does not mention Apuleius' description of the appearance of Isis to Lucius, he does similarly insist, on different grounds, that 'Pallas (Minerva), Artémis, Proserpine et Cérès n'étaient vraiment distinctes que dans la mythologie populaire'. All, he then goes on a page later, are Isis. Dupuis, Court de Gébelin, and others use the name Isis to describe the archetypal moon alongside the sun whom they call Hercules or Bacchus. As might be expected from them, the other goddesses contained in the composite nature-mother eye Emma from behind their attributes in certain key scenes. Indeed, having resolved to paint Emma as the 'type' of Isis, it seems that Flaubert planned to introduce into his text at some point all her component aspects, as later the correspondence shows him doing for Tanit (and Moloch) in *Salammbô*. Let us study three major examples.

The Greeks, it is said in Flaubert's *Saint Antoine*, sanctified humble features of daily life. 'On les possédait [the gods] dans sa maison et cette familiarité divinisait la vie.'[14] If this is borne in mind, an awareness of the multiple deity is perhaps acceptable in our first view of Les Bertaux, the farm where Emma lives with her father. Emphasis on Isis, evident in the rough drafts in the form of cows, both by sight and by sound, was excised from the final version: the hint must have seemed in the end much too obvious and singularly unsubtle to Flaubert—or perhaps to his friend and adviser Bouilhet. The more European Minerva's horses (of the sun), together with the *chatteries,* are singled out for comment instead (relevant otherwise too, as we have seen and shall see again). Hera's peacocks (less notably than in the rough drafts where the peacock 'fait la roue' before the peahen), Cybele's poultry, Isis' geese, Vesta's fire and fire-irons, Ceres' grain ('le trop-plein du grenier') will all be balanced later in the book by references sufficiently striking to seem part of Flaubert's contrived symmetry (the 'cri de paon' at the theatre, la mère Lefrançois at the inn, the geese referred to by the counsellor at the *Comices,* the temple of Vesta contemplated for Emma's tomb, the gleaning girl in the beggar's song). Furthermore, as at Emma's first meeting with Charles she bends over a sack of grain, and as later when she bends over the bowl of blood (rose-coloured in the *brouillon*)[15] as she makes Rodolphe's acquaintance, she evokes the first goddess of them all—commonly said to be the mother of Isis and Osiris—Nut, who will figure in *Salammbô* and be reproduced by

Salomé, as well as being figured in Creuzer's illustrations. Nut is again evoked for the third time in *Madame Bovary* by the blind man's song, which speaks of 'ma Nanette qui va s'inclinant/Vers le sillon qui nous les donne'. In one of Flaubert's contemporary sources, Isis was described in analogous terms as the goddess 'dont le corps embrasse l'espace immense des cieux ainsi que les planètes, les étoiles ... et dont la tête, les bras et les jambes touchent à la terre', that is, as Nut. Thus Flaubert has suggested her presence in the background in manifold form at Les Bertaux. The spacing of the trees in the farmyard further conjures up a colonnade, one of the many in *Madame Bovary* which seem to indicate a recurrent temple motif, beginning in a grove as the Celts had done—in the *pièce montée* which summons up a vision of evolving architecture through the ages, in the ruins at Banneville, the colour of which Flaubert hesitated over, deciding in the end on the brick shade he insisted elsewhere to be that of the Acropolis, in the town hall at Yonville with its Ionic columns, in the theatre at Rouen with its symmetrical balustrades. Finally, Emma's gravestone in the cemetery forms the climax of the series, its plans having included Hera's 'tronçon de colonne', Minerva's pyramid, a temple of Vesta, and 'une manière de rotonde', a representation of the globe and—albeit grotesquely—suggesting an equivalence between the *dea tella*, goddess of all nature, and Emma, goddess for Charles, in the Latin epitaph it bears: 'Sta viator' and 'amabilem conjugem calcas!'

In my second passage, the cardinal incident at La Vaubyessard, a hint to us of the presence of the 'déesse cachée' comparable with the portrait of Minerva at Les Bertaux is provided: a 'statue de femme, drapée jusqu'au menton, regardait la salle pleine de monde', where the main object of Emma's sacrilegious veneration is an aged debauchee courtier who had 'couché dans le lit des reines'. If we remember that the composite goddess has the moon as attribute and that Apuleius also describes her as moisture combined with warmth, the tableau that terminates with the statue again evokes her. There are its crystal and silver, both dedicated to the moon, the steam that rises, with its warm odours of luxury (steam is always present in Flaubert's scenes more than realism demands and is a recurrent motif in *Madame Bovary*), its flowers (Venus), bread (Ceres), quails (Isis) and *coquillages* (Proserpine)—these last still not reduced to the *homards* of the final version as late as the copyist's manuscript, when Flaubert finally realized how much more socially suitable lobsters would be for his tableau than the miscellaneous assortment of crustacea designated by the generic term first suggested to him by its connection with Proserpine. All these attributes of the great goddess will be echoed in further key scenes. All contribute acceptable details to a realistic picture, but all of them might just as well, if it were not for their attributive importance, have been replaced by others. Such a humble object as bread need not have been mentioned at all. Flaubert's aim is, as we know, plasticity, that is, visibility and concreteness, of which the first function is however to substantiate what he himself termed the 'idées' that were his point of departure. Thus the presence of Proserpine is further signalled (more conventionally and more recognizably) by Emma's initiation into the eating of pomegranates (as a result of which, in Ovid's *Metamorphoses*, Proserpine was never again able to escape wholly from the realm of Pluto). They will recur through the book in the form of the colour *grenat*. Alongside them are pineapples (the same shape as Dionysus' pine-cones that we later see in the seduction scene in the forest), accompanied by the fine white sugar that announces, as we know, the arsenic which will bring about Emma's death. One wonders indeed whether Ovid's account in the *Metamorphoses* of the rape of Proserpine through a great opening in the crust of the earth did not inspire the image used by Flaubert to describe the effect which La Vaubyessard has had upon Emma's life: 'un trou dans sa vie, à la manière de ces grandes crevasses qu'un orage, en une seule nuit, creuse quelquefois dans les montagnes.' Similarly, a further sense for the *ténèbres* and the darkness which invade Emma's consciousness in moments of frustration is revealed to us. We recognize that they are allusions to the Underworld and perceive that first Charles and now the *vicomte* who danced with her are in turn forms of its king. We remember also Flaubert's overall conviction, expressed in one of his earliest works, that 'l'enfer, c'est le monde'.[16] In this way, the evocation of Proserpine through her attributes has conveyed to us in plastic terms an aspect of Flaubert's philosophy and placed his representative human psyche against a background of general 'ideas' which lend fresh significance to the circumstances of her life and mark an irrevocable step in the advance of fatality. None of this is stated; all of it is shown through 'le fond'. Implicit is the knowledge that Flaubert gained from Plutarch as well as from Apuleius, namely, that 'Proserpine is Isis'.

My third representative scene is Flaubert's description of Emma's last night with Rodolphe in her garden at Yonville, a tableau which

Flaubert's printer Laurent-Pichat had attempted to simplify by removing certain images. In it, I have already identified Minerva, whom above all Emma has emulated, defied, offended. The ripe fruit of Ceres, the *belette* of Diana–Hecate, the scent of Venus' flowers, the shadows of Hera's *saules* widen the range of allusion. In particular, the spotted snake formed by the moonlight on the river is fascinating in its valencies. Not only did Flaubert refuse point-blank to remove it, not only can it be connected with Athene the snake goddess, it also evokes Proserpine and Diana, to both of whom the water snake was affected. The rough drafts show, moreover, that to associate the river with a serpent somewhere in the novel was one of Flaubert's aims; at least two other attempts in different places were abandoned.

Flaubert's water snake is headless and therefore sinister. *Madame Bovary* is a brutal book (for reasons we have seen), and 'l'élément brutal est au fond', Flaubert had reproachfully written to Laurent-Pichat with regard to the latter's attempted mutilations of this very passage.[17] The brutal element is not far to seek, for the sequence breathes a slow maturing of punishment and revenge on the part of the deities represented, always remembering that they are aspects of Nature. Perhaps, indeed, its main theme is that of harvest, foreshadowing the song of the blind man at Emma's death. Emma herself, although expecting to leave with Rodolphe on the morrow, feels a strange foreboding. Thus, the moon appearing at ground level to stare out from Flaubert's backcloth of natural scenery is 'toute ronde'. It has reached full term; its menacing colour is that of the sunset and the male, of blood and of wine. The swift parabola which it describes up into purity and dazzling whiteness traces in reverse, through tatters of blackness and light, the life of Emma, which had begun in just such virginal incandescence. The giant multiple torch thus formed drips starlight, silver, and diamantine crystals, all attributes of Minerva–Isis. The blackness of the night again recalls Latona whom we met at Banneville, mother of deadly Artemis and Apollo who may emerge out of the night even as do Bacchus and Venus from the foam. Latona was, moreover, pursued by a serpent at the moment of her giving birth. The silence of the scene (water does not, after all, usually flow absolutely in silence) presages a catastrophe and again is reminiscent of the abode of the dead. The breeze that blows carries to Emma–Psyche that *souffle* which, as she breathes it in, ministers physically to her soul, yet brings with it a current chill into the mild air. The flowing river, unchanging yet ever-renewed, confirms the eternal yet individual character of human feeling and of natural phenomena, stressing the uncontrollable motion of life and time, the energy of Hermes–Anubis ever at work on behalf of the great goddess, the mysterious impetus within the mechanism of Nature. Further movements bear witness to the inescapable hunting propensities of wild creatures hidden beneath the surface of natural beauty. Hecate, that other face of Diana, has begun her dread work. The repeated thud, soft but irreparable, of ripe fruit falling to the ground, seems to be the very sound of retribution. 'Je suis rond,' Lheureux will later say, coming to collect his matured debt.

And where Ceres is found, there is Proserpine. Flaubert's scaly snake whose head is not yet visible is followed by a reference to Emma whose voice first becomes 'enfantine' and who then addresses her lover as 'petit Rodolphe'. Thus Flaubert suggests that, just as after the *Comices* Rodolphe–Jupiter–Pistor had metaphorically coupled with Emma–Ceres to produce a new Emma, so now in the form of a spotted snake he has again figuratively united, as in Ovid's *Metamorphoses*, with this different Emma, the Proserpine whom he has transformed into 'quelque chose de souple et de corrompu', so that she may give birth to another form of Bacchus. The mother–son relationship between Emma and her lovers is being prepared, and a manifold nature for the water snake is hinted at.

The placing of the scene at a moment when Emma is on the point of making a great discovery about her lover and her life is thus richly suggestive. That Rodolphe was already signified to us at the *Comices* as speaking with a serpentine *sifflement* is brought into our minds. A further reason why Flaubert should have tried several times to insert the image and then been so adamant in retaining it is revealed. For in the belief of one of Flaubert's chief sources, Dupuis's *Origine des cultes*, the Hebrew serpent whom we earlier heard in Rodolphe's sibilants was heir to the great Persian evil principle Ahriman (mentioned in the correspondence), again a snake or dragon whose coming was described in the Persian cosmogony as the entry 'into the river' of the great *couleuvre*. Here is an undoubted source of Flaubert's image. Flaubert has been at pains to show us the time of the year also—September—the astronomical background and basis of such beliefs being as always discreetly present in his works. Winter is approaching, the cold which, since it means an absence of the opposite principle, the sun, the good in Sabeism, betokens in such a context the approach of evil. Emma's original seduction by Rodolphe in the forest had taken place in autumn; it is at the approach of winter that she will be taken by 'une grande ardeur musicale' and begin her affair with Léon.

Thus all these anthropomorphic and zoomorphic aspects of Nature have fused together in a richly ambiguous many-headed monster, visible within the very liquidity we earlier identified with love and with the powerful 'choses de ce monde', reproducing, moreover, one of Plato's own images for matter and for the life of the senses: the hydra. As so often, Emma is presented as at the same time victim and offender. Evil has entered her life and it also awaits her; neglect of her child (who was certainly not to have accompanied them, whatever Rodolphe's fears), physical infidelity, and the conviction that she can herself spin the web of her own life, will bring down upon her head the punishment and ironic justice which are Flaubert's chosen techniques of narration in this novel of antique fatality. Minerva and Proserpine, two of the key figures we have associated with the snake, come together in what Creuzer calls 'cette haute idée morale', *Praxidice*, which is usually indeed represented by a head. She is 'la déesse qui accomplit la justice, consomme la vengeance, mène à fin tout ce qui se dit et se fait, tire de toutes choses les dernières conséquences'. That Diana also has the water snake as attribute is again equally acceptable in a story concerning a woman who first impersonated one of Diana's amazons and then may be compared with Ariadne, for it was, according to Homer, Diana who punished with her arrows the wife of Theseus for preferring Dionysus, as Emma grows to do. Indeed, as Emma is dying, a heavy weight will seem to lie upon her tongue, just as Ariadne was pierced in the tongue by an arrow from the goddess.

This emphasis upon suspense and upon multiple possibilities about to be revealed brings us back to a consideration of the actual images that Flaubert had refused to remove from the passage, a snake and a candelabra. We realize that in fact Flaubert's landscape is here shadowing forth Emma–Psyche at the most decisive point in her story, that is, seeking, light in hand, to gaze on the face of the form of love. But Emma's vision will not be that of Psyche, who had feared to see a monster but found herself beholding the most beautiful of all wild things. She resembles much more the pregnant woman—so reminiscent of Isis—in *Revelations*: 'clothed in the sun, and the moon under her feet and upon her head a crown of twelve stars,' who is suddenly faced with another 'warden in heaven', a great dragon having seven heads and ten horns, a monster indeed. How many of the figures evoked by the deep structure of *Madame Bovary* have as their attribute a snake! Apollo's python and the serpent of Esculapius, not to speak of the hydra of Lerne, bring into the picture again the male sun, eternal quest of Emma, as we have seen. The sun, as well as the moon, is associated (in *Madame Bovary* as in legend) with arrows. Hidden within the clouds after Léon's departure, they are specifically identified with the rays of the hunting sun in the final scene with Rodolphe. The serpents of Ceres and of Isis remind us also that, besides being a constellation, the serpent is autochthonous, a creature of the earth, a fertility symbol. Typhon, who had dismembered the sun of Isis and Osiris, the great crocodile monster, another dragon, familiar to Flaubert from his Egyptian trip and from Creuzer, was, according to one legend, destroyed by her son Horus, the young sun. Isis herself relented, however, and permitted Typhon to live. For this, Horus tore from her brow her royal diadem. Hermes replaced it with the head of a cow, thus transforming her into the 'vache éternelle', for ever questing for the sun-god, as we have already seen her and as Flaubert portrays her in *Saint Antoine*.

In this guise, Isis is the very archetype of the moon, containing within her not only all the nature deities of whom the moon is attribute and whom we have seen Flaubert evoke in the text with Emma, but also the other female types, ancient and modern, whom we have recognized in the situations and yearnings which he has invented for her. Notable are the three Heliades, Pasiphaë and her daughters, Ariadne and Phaedra. The *serpent-taureau* that came out of the sea to destroy the innocent young sun Hippolytus (whose importance for *Madame Bovary* I have already shown) is Nature itself, Nature as the deadly moon, the half-serpent Melusine, the avatar of the 'éternel féminin' which in Flaubert does not redeem, Nature visualized as the equally eternal masculine, 'le taureau du soleil', also half-serpent in its form as Bacchus–Zagreus. Like Nature they are in truth both male and female. Both destroy as Charles and Emma destroy each other, named, as they both are, Bovary, as we have seen, a derisive version of the cow goddess, who is the bull of the Sun combined with the Moon. For the Flaubert from whom Nature had wrested in turn father, sister and friend, who recognized even as he buried his sister that out of such death comes life, the brutal irony of it all had to be accepted: 'Cela est, cela est',[18] then, through art, made bearable. Hence, at least in part, the farcical last syllable of the name of his two eternally representative protagonists: 'pour ce que rire est le propre de l'homme.'[19]

CHAPTER SIX

'A la hauteur du destin'

We have seen how Emma assumes the persona of the great goddesses, aspects of nature visualized as women. Since to seek even to
resemble the gods was, for the ancients, insolence, she is punished.
Psyche, the Heliades, and Eos were hounded by Venus; Arachne and
Iodamie by Minerva; Ariadne by Diana. Nature as vengeful is a concept familiar to Flaubert, who once described storms, catastrophes,
and pestilences as being means of correcting human beings in their
autolatrous presumption. Pythagoras had said that the various goddesses were aspects of woman's life—daughter, bride, mother. Emma
takes the history further, following in the steps of the inconstant
Venus.

In her relationship with the male, Emma falls victim to all but two
innocents—Charles and Justin—whom she in turn destroys. All,
including these two, have played in her life the role of the shape-shifter Hermes—Anubis, Psychopompus, messenger of the goddess,
bearer of souls from birth into death and associated with the Dionysus we have already identified. Emma's death being known to the
author before the telling of the story began—like that of Phèdre or of
Agamemnon—its approach is made incarnate in the individuals who
help bring it about, imparting to her life the quality of a tragic destiny.
Additional to the individuals are certain sounds, recurrent objects,
homonyms, personal characteristics, all combining to give to the narrative urgency, density, and above all resonances of infinite irony.

In his choice of details Flaubert draws not only upon Creuzer's
account of Hermes but also upon compilations by Maury, Langlois,
and Georges Kastner, giving historical surveys of traditional representations of the sight, sound, and attributes of the figure of Death.
Flaubert incorporated memories of his own earlier works, notably
his *Danse des morts* (1838) and the first version of *Saint Antoine*, as
well as items recorded in the *Notes de voyage*. Death as an allegorical

85

personage is far from new in Flaubert's literary output or preoccupations.

To start with Emma's father, he it was who took her to school, whose broken leg brought her in contact with Charles, who married her off to him for the sake of a reduced dowry although finding him rather 'gringalet', and thus, as Hermes did for Isis, bestowing upon her a bovine diadem or (always remembering the symbolism of the sun and the moon) enclosing her in a wooden case shaped like a cow after the fashion of the father in a story related by Creuzer which Flaubert at one time said he was thinking of taking as a subject. Finally, he appears at Emma's funeral, his face dyed blue like the face of 'Mercure le bleu' *(Saint Antoine)*,[1] stressing his function as he joins in the procession with the words: 'Je m'en vais la suivre jusqu'au bout.' The sensuous, comfort-loving heredity which he passed on to her is also implicit.

Charles, 'sauveur' of Emma's father, even more unknowing in his responsibility, first incarnates Hermes in his Egyptian form, Thoth, god of medicine, particularly connected with Isis already discerned behind Emma in Part One of the book. Place-names, says Creuzer, were not infrequently a personal name; place-names in Gaul, says Maury,[2] were often taken from divinities. The Egyptian associations in this part of the novel make one wonder whether Tostes (originally Tôtes in the scenarios) is not a dissimulated reference to Thoth.

Maxime du Camp brought back from Egypt a photograph of Isis wearing horns and moon disc and also one of Thoth crowned with a selection of spheres and circlets qualifying for Flaubert's comment in the *Notes de voyage*: 'exagération du symbolisme, coiffures très compliquées'[3] and perhaps partly the origin of Charles's comic headgear.

In his *Mémoire sur les personnages de la Mort,* Maury includes Thoth among the traditional representations of Death and this is, ironically and cruelly, what Charles is to Emma. Further examples in his list also suggest Charles—the horse of Death on which he came riding into Les Bertaux, already present in any case in Flaubert's own *Danse des morts* as well as in the first version of *Saint Antoine,* just as the whip which figures in the first scene between the young people—as again with Rodolphe in the seduction scene and on the wall of his room at the end of the book—was wielded by Death in the first *Saint Antoine* (the importance of the horse in *Madame Bovary* needs no stressing: it is still present in Emma's scene with Binet, whose lathe resembles 'les fers d'un cheval au galop', thus bringing together three major images—horse, dust, and wheels—in this incident). Then there are Charles's teeth which, Emma realizes just before the *pied bot* episode, 'ne sont point vilaines'. Rodolphe bares his when advancing masterfully upon Emma, while the organ-grinder bringing Emma 'échos du monde' is even more evocative of Death, 'la mâchoire reposant dans ses mains osseuses' in the *Danse des morts*.[4] All four men carry a knife, modern equivalent of the weapon worn by Death, Rodolphe to use in repairing a horse's bridle after the seduction scene, Léon for paring his nails, Homais for his pharmaceutical preparations, and Charles 'comme un paysan'. Charles's heavy boots resemble the footsteps of Death as derisively mentioned in *Bouvard et Pécuchet*, especially since the sound of approaching footsteps is feared by his first wife, Héloïse. But Death can also approach soundlessly, and the bailiff's clerk is shod with 'chaussons' as he listens to Emma's ancient piano, his 'feuille à la main'. The contrast heightens Charles's significance.

When the young couple move to Yonville, Isis would seem to have become Io (as in so many versions of the myth), for Emma is pregnant and has lost her dog. This strengthens the possibility that we have now moved to Greece, following hints contained in the Ionian columns of the town hall, the names Hippolyte and Artémise, and Homais's 'bonnet grec' which is stressed in juxtaposition with the Greek medical term *coryza*. The lion of Gaul giving its name to the local hostelry (emphasized in the *brouillon* in medieval *blason* form—'Lefrançois au lion d'or') was reputed by Celticists to be the imported lion of Ionia. If Léon bears the name, it is partly for this reason. Flaubert in a letter says that in character he was basically similar to Charles,[5] modern bearer of a royal name. Together they offer two versions of the nineteenth-century non-hero—a modern Apollo or Hercules (the lion is an attribute of the sun) and, as we have seen, one aspect of the modern Eros–Psyche. Both are also Hermes. Léon's part as Psychopompus is foreshadowed in the statue of the *Lion d'or* with its 'frisure de caniche'.

Homais in particular evokes Hermes, with his literary pretensions (Hermes invented letters as well as doctoring), his eloquence (already in the ancients and particularly present in Ogmios, the Celtic counterpart), his continual meddling, initiating fresh developments in the action. He it is who, in keeping with Creuzer's account of Hermes, announces the news of the approaching *Comices,* claiming to be an expert on agriculture as on everything else, and who inspires the *pied bot* operation (as Mme Lefrançois puts it, he was 'cause de tout'). He suggests the theatre to the 'heureux mortels' Charles and Emma, encourages Emma's music lessons—'il ne faut jamais laisser en friche les facultés de la nature'—interferes at the deathbed and is finally Psychopompus to Charles and to Berthe also, to whom, fittingly, he had been godfather (Hermes Psychopompus from birth until death). His sugary presents to her, his skill and impressiveness at the confection of rubicund jams, his revelation of the arsenic arising from this, connect him with Death as 'le piston de Dieu' in Langlois's list, while Maury cites the 'gardien de l'enfer' as *Apothecarius*. Brandishing a pair of scissors, he shears a lock of Emma's hair, breaking the skin: his wife is 'douce comme un mouton', discreetly implying that he himself possesses Hermes' own attribute, the *bélier*.

The name Homais, based upon *homo* according to one scenario,[6] thus evokes a human Hermes and underlines his importance as another manifestation of the masculine principle in its relationship with Emma. If Homais is noteworthy for his cowardice, this is in keeping with Flaubert's aims in writing his grotesque epic. All the 'heroes' in this novel share the 'lâcheté qui caractérise le sexe fort'. Their influence is none the less deadly. It is interesting that Homais should be marked with smallpox, closely associated, according to Maury, with traditional representations of Death.

Remaining still at Yonville, we note with a contemporary reviewer the resemblance between the reading and conversation of Emma and Léon and Dante's description of Paolo and Francesca. Already in this idyllic period the possibility of death and perhaps damnation lies in wait. 'L'enfer, c'est le monde' was in any case a theme of Flaubert's juvenilia, and at Tostes Emma's existence, 'morne et silencieuse', resembles Maury's account of souls in the Egyptian hell. When Léon leaves for Paris, Emma is again condemned to 'les mauvais jours de Tostes'.

Rodolphe, who rescues her temporarily, is described as *vir* in the scenarios.[7] A *chasseur*—ancient metaphor for Death—he lives at La Huchette, a name evocative of the hunting horn used to *hucher* (that is, call) in the death-hunt. It is in his glibness of tongue that Rodolphe, like Lheureux, directly resembles Hermes. Together with Lheureux, Rodolphe, incorporating the serpent in his composite figure, can also be seen as one of those monsters, half man and half beast, which, in Maury's list, figure the vengeful Furies or Eumenides (Flaubert

makes Emma, otherwise unaccountably, terrified of meeting
Rodolphe in Rouen). Lheureux's very name is now explained if we
remember that the Greek word Eumenides is a euphemism for
Erinnyes (the Bad Ones) and itself means 'the Happy Ones'. Certainly he pursues and hunts down Emma, a fury in the guise of a
servitor, from the moment in which, Djali–Anubis having disap-
peared, he steps instead out of the coach with tales of dogs finding
their way from as far as Constantinople. By Part Three, so much of
which takes place in Rouen of which one derivation is 'house of the
Romans', Hermes–Mercury, Roman god of commerce and thieves, is
his fitting patron, his *alter ego* another dog, 'ce mâtin de Vinçart'.
Both dogs and serpents were associated with the Furies. Lheureux it
is who is largely responsible for inspiring in Emma a liking for lies
and deception as Hermes had in that other form of the first woman,
Pandora, who also had begun his career with the blessing of Minerva,
who was also god of all species of 'profit personnel', the significance
of which in *Madame Bovary* Professor Fairlie has shown.[8] Like
Death, Lheureux reads out a register of Emma's debts. He is capable
of mental calculations 'à effrayer Binet même', whose actual profes-
sion is concerned with the working out of dues.

Binet, the importance of whose lathe in this delicately devised tale
of fate and retribution we have noticed, first appears in the role of
that attribute of Death, silence—the fish (the *alose*) with which he is
compared indicating his function as envoy of the goddess, to whom
the fish was affected. His respect for time is as remarkable as Hivert's
memory. As huntsman and at the same time a *diablotin*, he frightens
and is offended by Emma, appearing immediately afterwards in a
scene of weighing and measuring with Homais, which in the circumstances—an agitated Emma is present—seems to presage one of the
psychostasia, or Hermes weighing souls in the balance, of which
Maury had written another historical survey and which Creuzer
includes in his illustrations. Measuring—*l'aunage*—is also one of the
activities of Lheureux.

Grotesque and horrifying example of Hermes, a vision of his face
to be Emma's accompaniment on her final journey into the *ténèbres,*
the blind beggar is the version which Flaubert allows Emma of the
groom we have seen her longing for. Carrying, like Hermes, a stick,
he has from the beginning been associated with travel and wheeled
vehicles and provides with *épouvantement* the final manifestation of
a form of terror recurring throughout the story, initiated by Homais's

'expression congrue' to describe the news of le père Tellier's ruin—
'quelle épouvantable catastrophe!'—and reiterated in the death
chamber: 'jamais le pharmacien n'avait cru qu'il pût y avoir de si
épouvantable spectacle.' Linked by Creuzer with Dionysus, *épou-
vante* provides a further instance of the overlapping and thus basic
unity of themes for Flaubert.

The *comédie* which Hivert obliges the blind beggar to perform
reveals him as part dog, in keeping (as in the case of Lheureux) with
the Anubis element in Hermes as well as with the suggestion of the
Erinnyes, that is of another 'monster', part human and part beast.
The scales around the beggar's eyes evoke a third element (Rodolphe
the wolf is, like Lheureux, also tripartite), an Egyptian crocodile,
attribute which Athene–Neith had transported to Athens. Before
Flaubert had decided on the details he had in fact, in accordance
with his practice of starting with generalities and then finding the
exact forms later, planned the apparition of a *monstre* of some kind,
originally to emerge from the Bois-Guillaume (where formerly there
was a temple to Venus). The *idea* of a monster thus came before
precision. (Salammbô's later affirmation in her invocation to the
goddess—'c'est par toi que se produisent les monstres'[9]—may well be
significant.) The suggestion of an approaching monster is also
present in the text—together with so much else—in the description of
Rouen Cathedral where the window of the Gargouille shows the
famous *serpent-dragon* mentioned by Hugo in the *Préface de
Cromwell* (and which, according to Langlois, had also dwelt in the
abode of Venus). Forms of the word *gargouiller,* as well as early
mentions of the creature itself, appear in Flaubert's scenarios and
rough drafts, and eventually two are retained in the final text (both in
Rouen), as though to stress the sound and herald its impending
arrival with the symmetry which Flaubert felt necessary. A dragon
similarly appears among the fireworks at the *Comices.* Flaubert's
letter to Bouilhet reveals that the monster had at first been intended
to be both legless, a 'cul de jatte',[10] and to evoke something foreshadowed by Hugo's 'culs-de-jatte qui ressemblent à des limaces'.
Bouilhet refers to the blind beggar as 'ton troisième',[11] indicating, I
suggest, that Rodolphe and Lheureux were two monsters already
included. That the last prefiguration of Death in Emma's life should
be blind, places him in a long tradition which includes Ovid, as
Flaubert might have read in Langlois.

It is in his song that the blind beggar is perhaps most significant for the theme in *Madame Bovary* of the impact of masculine upon feminine, of human alongside natural. It resumes Emma's life.

> Souvent la chaleur d'un beau jour
> Fait rêver fillette à l'amour.
> Pour amasser diligemment
> Les épis que la faux moissonne
> Ma Nanette va s'inclinant
> Vers le sillon qui nous les donne.
> Il souffla bien fort ce jour-là,
> Et le jupon court s'envola!

'La chaleur d'un beau jour' evokes Emma with Charles at Les Bertaux and outside the theatre, Emma walking along the riverside with Léon, Emma at the *Comices* with Rodolphe (and Lheureux), Emma in the woods with Rodolphe ('Dieu nous protège'), Léon awaiting Emma near the Cathedral in Rouen, all scenes inaugurating Emma's particular adventures in love. The word 's'inclinant' reminds us how we have twice seen Emma bending over—first with Charles to retrieve his 'nerf de bœuf', next (most sinister as we now realize) to pick up a bowl of blood in her first encounter with Rodolphe. Emma's activity and the notion of ploughing and reaping are in the song, with memories of the wind which has blown throughout the book: Emma gazing through the farmhouse window at the havoc wrought by a storm in the garden, for instance, or refreshing herself in the night breeze at the window in La Vaubyessard; the frightening 'rafales de vent' bringing the scent of the salt sea to Banneville; Homais discoursing on 'des brises de Russie'; peasant bonnets fluttering at the *Comices;* wind in the dry reeds, in the leaves or the bare branches during the love-scenes beneath the 'tonnelle'; the fragments of Emma's torn letter gathered up by a gust and scattered; the wind blowing in the 'vasistas' of the *Hirondelle;* the 'coup de vent' that blew away the clouds from her brow when Léon tells her of his love; and the figurative *tourbillons* and *ouragans* which have howled in the depths of Emma's consciousness, from the 'insaisissable malaise' of Tostes to the sound of the beggar's own voice near the *Hirondelle* in Rouen.

Emma's shriek of ironic laughter shows that she has understood the song. Most brutal of all (the word which, as I have said elsewhere, is Flaubert's own concerning the book in general), is the last line: 'Et le jupon court s'envola.' For Emma, in her social presumption, has always worn her skirts very long—her wedding-dress (from which

Charles passively allowed her to pluck the 'chardons'), the riding-habit (from which Rodolphe actively held back the bracken), the 'dentelles de sa jupe' which vied in Léon's esteem with the 'exaltation de son âme', skirts blue, yellow, black, flowing, flounced, rustling in a silken *frou-frou,* but never the peasant garb worn by Nanette, to whom, however, she now recognizes her resemblance.

The beggar's voice is 'rauque'; earlier, 'aiguë'. It had been set in counterpart against the moving coach—'la sonnerie des grelots, le murmure des arbres et le ronflement de la boîte creuse'—and thus incorporated in the manifold sounds which have orchestrated the approach of self-destruction in this dance of Life and Death. Flaubert's early *Danse des morts* is significant for *Madame Bovary* in that the Death Dance is actually referred to in it as a waltz. There the dead have 'ongles longs, polis, blanchis',[12] a confirmatory gloss on Emma's activity as she transforms herself into the Northern white witch, the *fantôme* who, after death, will be for Charles and Berthe the harpy Ceres–Proserpine. In this work of Flaubert also, Death is designated 'ce joyeux ménétrier',[13] putting us in mind of the violinist leading Emma's wedding procession, 'serpentant' on its initiatory way. Her music-master earlier at school, we learn in a flashback, had also played the violin. Hyacinthe Langlois, Flaubert's teacher of drawing to whom he owed so much, wrote a history of Dances of Death, posthumously published in 1852 and known to have been in Flaubert's library,[14] which was followed closely by a more complete study by Georges Kastner.[15] The latter in particular stresses the sounds and musical instruments traditionally associated with the approach of Death, complementing the lists given by Langlois and Maury of traditional visual representations. Included in Kastner's list are not only the *sistre* and the *tringles* and rattles which we have heard already but a hunting-horn called a *huchet,* a portable barrel-organ slung over the shoulder, keyboards, stringed instruments (Emma's piano is referred to in these terms), bagpipes *(Lucie de Lammermoor),* trumpets (hence *la Renommée*—mentioned by Kastner—in la mère Rolet's kitchen, sounding the first alarm), flutes (opera and Léon), a trombone (the masked ball), a mandoline (as in Léon's Paris room alongside the 'tête de mort'), *cornets à piston* (Dodolphe 'et tout le tremblement'), a tambourine ('Berthe tambourinait sur la fenêtre'), drums—a *grosse caisse* for example (the closing of the shutter as signal to the waiting Charles and all the banging on doors by Hivert and by Charles as in the *bac* on the return journey from La

Vaubyessard, leading to the hammering down of the coffin, and finally the 'cailloux' descending upon it), not to speak of a 'charivari' of noise, Flaubert's own word to describe the orchestra in *Lucie,* and the *serpent,* booming at Emma's funeral ceremony. Most telling of all Kastner's illustrations, suggesting even more strongly that Flaubert knew the book, shows Death offering a toy windmill to a child, even as Berthe Bovary is suddenly shown carrying one. An example of overlapping imagery, it combines the all-important wheel (including all the weather-vanes) with the wind which played its part in the blind man's song, that is, with the *souffle* of Maury's Death (one of Maury's list), associated with Hermes (Creuzer) and personified by the Eumenides (Maury).

All these medieval as well as Classical notations have been used by Flaubert to deepen and enrich the narrative with motifs which appeal in secret to memories, fears, prejudices, superstitions, artistic traditions, and make their effect unknown to the reader. They help explain a remark of Flaubert's which greatly impressed Théophile Gautier: 'de la forme naît l'idée',[16] interesting when set alongside Flaubert's assertions that the major aim of poetry is plasticity. Having decided to tell a story in the manner of a literary genre—in this case the *Danse des morts,* earlier the grotesque epic and the *mystère*—he then arrived at incidents, characters, and visual details which gave flesh (physical appearance and oral expression) to ideas first arising from the literary form. In this category we may further place a traditional part of the *Danse des morts,* the 'Débat du Corps et de l'Ame', in the form of the comic discussion between Homais and Bournisien, seated beside the dead body of Emma. To laugh at the grim, an essential feature of the medieval Dances of Death, was also for Flaubert a sign of strength and an aim in itself.

Other examples culled from Flaubert's sources include Death figured as a 'bonhomme noir'. This occurs some four times. First in the person of the organ-grinder, with his dark face, his circular dances, and his monkey (in Egypt consecrated to the moon-goddess); secondly as Bournisien enters the *Lion d'or,* an 'homme vêtu de noir' who makes Mme Lefrançois 'tressaillir' and will be far from absolved of responsibility for Emma's downfall; thirdly in Rodolphe's 'visage hâlé' which, alongside the fourth example, Lheureux's complexion resembling 'une concoction de réglisse', suggests a personage mentioned by both Langlois and Kastner, namely Arlequin. With his blackened face, suspect morality, and composite clothing, Arlequin seems clearly present in Rodolphe, while Lheureux, combining Gascon and Norman, is also composite. That Flaubert wished in his by now familiar method to mention the word which describes them somewhere in the text and thus insinuate it into our minds may perhaps be deduced from the slang term *chicard,* which is part of Homais's vocabulary when he affects 'le genre artiste', taking up an earlier, suppressed description of the life of artistes as 'bariolée comme un habit arlequin'. Thus a further tradition of representing both the male as a type and Death emerges, that of the Commedia dell'Arte.

All extend the picture of the female in contact with the male of which the most deadly form is the arsenic which killed Emma, its etymology, as we have seen, being 'male'. But arsenic, as Flaubert knew, is semi-metallic, for he once approved an arsenic cure being followed by a friend with the words: 'Il *faut* boire du fer.'[17] Here we are on the fringe of another network of images relative to our subject and for which I shall again take as my departure-point the song of the blind beggar. In it there is mention of the 'épis que la faux moissonne', the scythe being the beggar's equivalent of the cutting edge carried by other characters as well as a customary attribute of Death and Time. All may be taken as having relevance to Maury's figure of Death as 'le fer qui tranche'. Metal, in particular iron, has recurred in noteworthy circumstances. The streams at Yonville flow over ferruginous rocks. We have heard metal in the *sistre,* the *tringles,* and the rattles. Then there is Rodolphe's letter, crackling in Emma's hand 'comme une plaque de tôle', the cast-iron steeple, modern addition to Rouen Cathedral, which seemed to Léon to be aspiring his whole love, the 'bruit assourdissant' heralding the future of Berthe, and the 'vapeur métallique' which covers the perspiring face of Emma as the poison begins to do its work.

And thus, as we read, the realization that this emerging industrial society in the background of *Madame Bovary* is indeed for Flaubert, as for Langlois, 'l'âge de fer' come upon us. The Dance of Death is another way of viewing the epic and the *mystère,* as, in similar circumstances, it was for Edgar Allan Poe. Like Ovid's *Metamorphoses* or Creuzer's *Symbolique* or an 'Orphic' cosmogony, the novel has spun an unbroken thread from the earliest times to the present day. Homais's apotheosis, owing so much to his 'uncle', is evocative of even the end of Ovid's *Metamorphoses,* as Charles's ultimate resignation is reminiscent of Ovid's description of the iron age, largely repeated by Flaubert's dying Jupiter in *Saint Antoine*. Relevant also is Flaubert's decision to include the cylindrical Rouen cakes called *cheminots*—'puisque j'ai la prétention de *peindre* Rouen'.[18] Having failed to introduce to his satisfaction in various drafts a reference to an 'employé de chemin de fer',[19] he includes instead objects of which the name is a homonym (Sartre, as well as the correspondence, has shown Flaubert's liking for the pun). An allusion to the iron way upon which the world was embarked and which had by now come to Rouen, as the progress of the *fiacre* which calls at the station reflects, is perhaps intended.

That the lives of Charles and Emma had been presented in terms of roads is undoubted—Charles continually on horseback; the 'petit sentier' of Charles's life; Emma leaving her illusions and hopes 'à toutes les auberges de la route'. We also know that Flaubert would all his life hate railways—'quelle turpitude!' And then he is able to include in the spectacle of Mme Homais crunching 'héroïquement' these 'têtes de mort'—'malgré sa mauvaise dentition'—an allusion to the approach of Death (towards Berthe for instance) as a 'vieille édentée', one of the metaphors in his own early Dance of Death. But perhaps the greater part of his secret reason for introducing the *cheminots,* at this point in composition when he also wrote to Bouilhet that he was really enjoying 'le fond', came from his personal memory of seeing an object resembling a *cheminot* during his Eastern voyage.[20] Let it not be thought that anything would consciously be introduced by Flaubert for self-indulgent or picturesque reasons foreign to the text. 'Il faut ainsi que tout sorte du sujet.'[21] The article cited by Flaubert in the *Notes de voyage* is a hat being worn by none other than the shape-shifting male Hermes, the Psychopompus we have already met.

Lestiboudois with his *pioche* and his rake (especially in a scene with Berthe) begins in the context of the Dance of Death to appear sinister, the *batelier* with his *aviron*, heralded by the fishermen and their baskets in the Cathedral stained-glass windows likewise, while the reason for the inclusion of hammering and the smell of *goudron* in an idyll of young love in the port of Rouen stands revealed, presaging the stench of smoke and of sin in the novels of François Mauriac. Another circle of hell is in the offing. Thus those readers with Classical knowledge recognize the goddesses, Dionysus and Hermes; others respond with folk memories or with elements of their own religious training. None of these 'profound and intimate recognitions', as Jung has said of primordial images, need in fact be consciously formulated. All contribute to the secret power of *Madame Bovary;* most were deliberately contrived by Flaubert.

Among all the men in Emma's entourage, the responsibility of the youngest, Justin, for her end is, next to that of Charles, the most touching and ironic. Camillus or some ephebe in the Classical setting, 'petit frère' and expert climber of trees in the context of Emma's youthful reading (*Paul et Virginie*), 'bel enfant' announcing Death in Maury's list, example of the Norman belief cited by Langlois in a Death which 'vient graisser nos bottes pour le dernier voyage', he it is who provides Emma with the key to the cupboard which holds the poison. In him, as in Charles, is shown the adoration of a dominating woman bringing with her nothing less than death, followed in Justin's case by what we take was for Flaubert a kind of death in life.

Flaubert's known fondness for puns found support in the presence of plays upon words in some of his models—Ovid's rhymes or the jokes which enlivened the Medieval Death Dances. It lends confirmation to the conviction that many of the relevant motifs in *Madame Bovary* may also be seen as homonyms, the device being yet another means of imparting multivalency to metaphors and establishing coincidence between them. The manifold forms of the verbs *rouler, tourner, filer,* and *ronfler,* together with personal- and place-names, the colour and substance *vermeil,* have provided examples. I shall confine myself here to examining two further instances relevant to the theme—the various forms of the word *pique* and Dr Larivière's 'calembour inaperçu'.

With the words *pique* and *piquer* we are simultaneously in the domain of Minerva (whose lance in the many illustrations included by Creuzer is always called a *pique*), of Death as 'le fer qui tranche', and of the Northern myths in which *les épines* allegorically bring about death. Flaubert's method, of which I have already shown something, is to use a word in a number of senses on a number of occasions in order to impress the sound upon us. Thus if *pique* occurs with its most common signification when Emma pricks her fingers at her sewing and again on a 'fil de fer' in her wedding bouquet, or when Léon buys cactus plants, Binet says of the cold weather (the elements are repeatedly shown to be present in the background of *Madame Bovary*): 'ça pique.' Emma's father uses the Normandism *picots* to describe Charles's annual reward, which will go on after Emma's death; the *pied bot* operation is, so Homais declares, 'une simple piqûre'; a 'piqûre de la lancette' initiates the 'saignée' which causes Emma to meet Rodolphe; Emma suffers from 'picotements' when she faints after the masked ball in Rouen, Mme Caron likewise when she consults Dr Larivière; Homais, as he cuts a lock of her hair for Charles (with scissors like the Parcae), 'tremblait si fort qu'il piqua la peau des tempes en plusieurs places'.

Épines occur frequently: on the road as Charles rides to Les Bertaux; in the garden at Tostes; le père Rouault's letter cackles like a 'poule à demi-cachée dans une haie d'épines'; Charles at Emma's funeral procession walks between hedges of 'épine', so much of what he passes an ironic echo of earlier episodes in his life with 'Elle'. In several scenarios la mère Rolet was shown waiting behind a hedge of 'épine', intended perhaps as an allusion to the spinning wheel and the death of Aurora. Spines figure not only on Léon's cactuses (there is another cactus in Guillaumin's house) but on those at La Vaubyessard which resemble 'des nids de serpents', a simile in which *épines* and serpents, both symbols of the approach of winter, seem to have been brought deliberately together, the thorns and needles of the Northern solar myths meeting Creuzer's 'serpent de l'automne' which is also the 'serpent de la mort'. How often in *Madame Bovary* cardinal events relating to Emma's life and loves take place in autumn—Charles's proposal, the visit to La Vaubyessard, the onset of Emma's feeling for Léon, Rodolphe's reappearance after the *Comices*, Emma's illness, her 'grande ardeur musicale' leading to her visits to Rouen! In one instance, that of Charles's proposal to Emma, the season is specifically referred to as 'à l'époque de la Saint-Michel', a notation confirming my overall view of the significance for Emma of the men who enter her life. St Michael, says Maury, seems proved to have been Hermes Psychopompus, introduced into Christian dogmas under this name, his attributes including the weighing-scales that I have already shown to be part of Flaubert's allegory.

The solar metaphor I have described in the background of *Madame Bovary* thus acquires new resonances. Like Lheureux, the composite Rodolphe who already has the wolf in his name incorporates the serpent. An equivalence is being established between the effect of certain men upon Emma and that of winter cold, Death, and, it would now appear, if never openly stated, evil. Flaubert's ideas in general on evil are another subject: let us simply note here in *Madame Bovary* the invocation at the Opera to 'l'ange du mal' (a scene invented or imperfectly remembered by Flaubert),[22] the application to Lheureux of the word *éternel* ('je suis éternel,' says Satan in *La Danse des morts*)[23] and, in connection with the whole theme of the age of iron and the pricking and wounding with a metal point, Plutarch's remark that 'iron is the bone of Typhon', that is, the Egyptian crocodile god of evil. What better indication, perhaps, of the long-established unity in Flaubert's mind of all our recent themes than the interest he showed during the Egyptian journey in identifying Creuzer's 'Typhon musicien'?[24]

There remains Dr Larivière's 'calembour inaperçu'.

Enfin, M. Larivière allait partir, quand Madame Homais lui demanda une consultation pour son mari. Il s'épaississait le sang à s'endormir chaque soir après le dîner.
—Oh! ce n'est pas le *sens* qui le gêne.
Et, souriant un peu de ce calembour inaperçu, le docteur ouvrit la porte.

Some external help towards understanding the equivalence *sang/ sens* may come from *Saint Antoine* in which the decadent Hercules complains of his strength: 'ma force m'étouffe, c'est le sang qui me gêne,' and longs to sit and spin at the feet of Omphale. Ogmios the Celtic Hermes was also identified by Romans with Hercules, and it is another inadequate modern version of a former hero that Flaubert is portraying in Homais who, for the 'besoins de son commerce', was capable of extreme cowardice and disloyalty.

Of the remarks made by the critics I have found most help and relevance in Pierre Danger's conclusion that in Flaubert's novels blood and its colour are regularly associated with the male and with violent death.[25] This is particularly apparent in *Salammbô*, where red is the colour of Moloch, but in *Madame Bovary* too blood is part of the menace of virile sexuality. Let us consider some of the uses of the word *sang* in the text.

A first group of examples links blood to the theme of the *piqûre*, the significance of which we have seen above—Emma sucks her pricked finger, blood flows when Berthe gashes her cheek, Hippolyte bleeds when Charles operates on his club foot, and Charles's medical methods involve much bleeding: 'Charles recevait au visage le jet tiède des saignées', 'il vous saignait les gens largement, comme des chevaux'. It is on the occasion of a *saignée* that Rodolphe and Emma meet, and we see her bending over a bowl of blood. The technique of homonymy comes into play when, after Emma's wedding, we are told of 'des carrioles emportées qui couraient au grand galop, bondissant dans les saignées', with the noteworthy additional detail that women are desperately trying to retrieve the reins. Another group brings out the sense of threat and horror in the thought of blood. The blind beggar's eyes are depicted as 'deux orbites tout ensanglantées', and almost immediately afterwards light filtered through red curtains covers the travellers in the *Hirondelle* with 'des ombres sanguinolentes'. During her mad rush home after Rodolphe has refused to help her, Emma is conscious only of 'le battement de ses artères, qu'elle croyait entendre s'échapper comme une assourdissante musique qui emplissait la campagne', and feels her soul slipping away from her 'comme les blessés, en agonisant, sentent l'existence qui s'en va par leur plaie qui saigne'. It is no surprise that on Emma's deathbed 'elle ne tarda pas à vomir du sang', just as Charles's first wife Héloïse had died after coughing blood.

Closely connected with blood is *rougeur*. Blood may rise to the face, causing a red blush, often linked with sexual embarrassment, as when Emma goes red after handing Charles his riding-crop on their first meeting, when Charles himself has red cheeks because of her proximity, when she blushes during her visit to la mère Rolet with Léon, and when, on Léon's departure, 'un flot de sang lui courut sous la peau, qui se colora tout en rose'. On other occasions, the redness comes from a fire or from warmth. On first arriving at the *Lion d'or,* Emma is suffused with 'une grande couleur rouge' from the fireplace, and later she takes pleasure in making the tongs red-hot in her own fireplace. One is reminded of this when Emma goes to implore Guillaumin to advance her money: she is received by a servant wearing a red waistcoat, the room is extremely hot, and when Guillaumin tries to seduce her 'un flot de pourpre' mounts to her cheeks. This redness of anger is matched by Homais's indignation when Justin takes the key to his *capharnaüm* and he is said to be 'plus rubicond que les groseilles'. Berthe's impending death is adumbrated by 'des plaques rouges aux pommettes'.

Red objects occur frequently, often with sinister connotations. A whole collection of red flowers is evoked, nearly all poisonous: foxgloves and poppies at Banneville, geraniums at Les Bertaux and in Emma's house after her death, while the fragments of the torn-up letters thrown from the cab containing Emma and Léon are shown against a background of 'un champ de trèfles rouges tout en fleur'. Red fruit is present: the 'groseilles' of the jam-making which is taking place when the existence of the arsenic is revealed, the cherries of the garden at Tostes. The escarpment near Yonville is streaked with 'de longues traînées rouges' from rainwater. The setting sun is red again and again: during Charles's studies in Rouen, just before the trip to La Vaubyessard, at Emma's vain attempt to seek solace from Bournisien, at Rodolphe's first visit to her after the *Comices,* during the seduction in the woods, and when Emma and Léon are together in Rouen. This stress on the seeming death of the sun recalls the solar mythology discussed in an earlier chapter and so prominent in *Salammbô.*

In *Madame Bovary* Love and Death have thus advanced hand in hand. Both, says Hesiod, are born of the night, his myth conveying in set form what happened when, summoned out of the darkness by a word from Emma, Charles set forth towards Les Bertaux, guided by the moon herself as in a folk-tale or symbolist story. Charles–Eros has become Charles–Thanatos. But Emma has also become Proserpine. Her nature as a harpy has been indicated by Flaubert even before her death, which brings that of Charles in its wake—first, when her voice singing Lamartine's *Le Lac* evokes the fluttering of wings, secondly when her very feet in their swansdown slippers are shown as winged, thirdly when she is feared as a siren, a *monstre* inhabiting the depths of love. That is indeed just what she has been for Charles, and, though Léon escapes her, the fears of his mother, who sees her in this light, are in Flaubert's world of ambiguity at one and the same time laughable and justified. Perhaps this unflinching book does produce a kind of catharsis in the reader, in that one feels pity for the powerless characters and terror at their peculiarly brutal fate. But it is with the comic as well as deadly Homais that the work ends. We are to be left with laughter rather than tears, though it is a singularly bitter and mirthless laughter.

POSTFACE

According to a manuscript plan of the book, Chapter Seven, entitled *L'Âge de raison* ('avec la *Bovary* finie, c'est l'âge de raison qui commence'), would have dealt with *Salammbô* and *L'Éducation sentimentale*. In an untitled Chapter Eight, *La Tentation de saint Antoine, Trois Contes,* and *Bouvard et Pécuchet* would have been discussed, after which would have come a general conclusion under the title *The Saving Eros*.

In the incomplete draft of the section on *Salammbô*, Margaret Lowe shows how aspects of the masculine–feminine antithesis implicit in *Madame Bovary* are brought out openly in the later novel, with its stress on the male principle of Moloch and the female principle of Tanit, and she examines the similarities and differences between the Norman housewife and the Carthaginian princess, both of them obsessed with the idea of the mystic marriage. She also analyses the parallels between the signs of imminent collapse in Carthage and the symptoms of decadence Flaubert detected in nineteenth-century France. Unfortunately, though she had done much preparatory work on the later writings, notably *L'Éducation sentimentale,* there is no means of knowing exactly how she proposed to work out her ideas on them, even if the general lines of her argument are already clear. *Hérodias* is the exception here; she saw it as a key work of Flaubert's latter years and had published several penetrating studies on it, bringing out not only the conflict of male and female principles which it exemplifies with particular sharpness, but also the extent to which, in its antique setting, it is an oblique but devastating comment on society in the Industrial Age (which is why she called it a 'roman du Second Empire').

These various threads would have been brought together in the final chapter, in which she intended to develop the theme of the masculine–feminine pattern underlying all that Flaubert wrote, linking it both with the eternal in myth and with the contingent in his view of the civilization of his own time. Thus she would have demonstrated the essential but hidden unity of Flaubert's thought and of his creative processes, and would have opened up a whole new way to the understanding of his works.

   Though it is profoundly to be regretted that Margaret Lowe did
not live to complete this book, enough of the lines of her thought
have emerged in that part of it which was finished for every reader to
be able to construct his own continuation of them for the remaining
novels. Flaubert always argued that the effect of the best writing was
to 'faire rêver'; there can be little doubt that that is what she has done
for everyone who cares about his novels.

A. W. RAITT

Notes

Preface

1. *Œuvres complètes,* Paris, Club de l'Honnête Homme, 1971–6, vol. 13, p. 365 (further references to this edition will be given in abbreviated form, thus: 13, p. 365).
2. 16, p. 310.
3. 13, p. 233.
4. 2, p. 144.
5. See Jean Bruneau, *Le 'Conte oriental' de Flaubert,* Paris, 1973.
6. 2, p. 449.
7. 12, p. 49.
8. 14, p. 603.
9. 13, p. 581.

Chapter One

1. 12, p. 148.
2. 13, p. 225.
3. *Souvenirs intimes,* in Flaubert, *Correspondance,* vol. I, Paris, 1926, p. xl.
4. *Les Romanciers naturalistes,* Paris, 1895, p. 208. See also 16, p. 224.
5. 13, p. 612.
6 13, p. 77.
7. 4, p. 126.
8. 15, p. 133.
9. Frédéric Creuzer, *Les Religions de l'antiquité considérées principalement dans leurs formes symboliques et mythologiques,* translated by J.-D. Guignault, 10 vols., Paris, 1825–51.
10. *Œuvres,* Paris, 1938, vol II, p. 450.
11. 12, p. 588.
12. 10, p. 44.
13. 13, p. 438.
14. *Essais,* Paris, 1950, p. 222.
15. 13, p. 438.
16. See *Correspondance Flaubert–Sand,* ed. Alphonse Jacobs, Paris, 1981.
17. 13, p. 482.
18. See Flaubert, *Correspondance,* ed. Jean Bruneau, Paris, 1973– (two volumes published so far).
19. *Œuvres,* vol. II, p. 643.
20. Ibid., p. 448.
21. 13, p. 655.
22. 13, p. 272.
23. *Souvenirs d'enfance et de jeunesse,* Paris, 1953, pp. 49–51.
24. 15, p. 517.
25. *Souvenirs intimes,* p. xl.

26. 15, p. 446.
27. Ibid..
28. 14, p. 111.
29. 12, p. 49.
30. 13, p. 229.
31. 13, p. 349.
32. 14, p. 409.
33. 12, p. 511.
34. 13, p. 317.
35. 13, p. 567.
36. 13, p. 158.
37. 13, p. 236.
38. 13, p. 380.
39. 13, p. 236.
40. 13, p. 222.
41. 14, p. 203.
42. 13, p. 158.
43. 14, p. 20.
44. 13, p. 439.
45. 13, p. 585.
46. 15, p. 430.
47. 13, p. 402.
48. *Œuvres*, vol. II, p. 449.
49. Preface to *Correspondance entre Gustave Flaubert et George Sand,* Paris, 1884, p. xvii.
50. 12, p. 47.
51. 13, p. 541.
52. 15, p. 439.
53. 13, p. 541.
54. 16, p. 310.
55. 14, p. 53.
56. 13, p. 268.
57. 15, p. 288.
58. 12, p. 437.
59. 13, p. 390.
60. *The Novels of Flaubert,* Princeton, 1966, p. 125.
61. 13, p. 314.
62. 14, p. 353.
63. 13, p. 438.
64. 13, p. 314.
65. 12, p. 554.
66. *Préface de Cromwell,* ed. Maurice Souriau, Paris, n.d., p. 183.
67. 15, p. 129.
68. *Préface de Cromwell,* p. 186.
69. *'Madame Bovary', Nouvelle Version,* ed. Jean Pommier and Gabrielle Leleu, Paris, 1949, p. 493.
70. *Préface de Cromwell,* p. 202.
71. 12, p. 346.
72. *Préface de Cromwell,* p. 207.
73. 12, pp. 1–23.
74. *Œuvres,* vol. II, p. 449.
75. 4, p. 259.
76. 12, p. 343.

77. 12, p. 569.
78. 13, p. 375.
79. 12, p. 533.
80. 12, pp. 50–1.
81. 13, p. 166.
82. 13, p. 375.
83. 12, p. 527.
84. 13, p. 136.
85. 12, p. 49.
86. 13, p. 331.
87. 13, p. 323.
88. 15, p. 570.
89. 13, p. 554.
90. 13, p. 185.
91. 13, p. 331.
92. 5, p. 138.
93. 15, p. 478.
94. 8, p. 440.
95. 8, p. 262.

Chapter Two

1. 13, p. 675.
2. 13, p. 290.
3. 14, p. 217.
4. 13, p. 116.
5. 10, p. 582.
6. 13, p. 461.
7. See *Le Christ aux Oliviers*, in *Œuvres*, Paris, vol. I, 1956, p. 38.
8. H. B. Riffaterre, *L'Orphisme dans la poésie romantique*, Paris, 1970, pp. 71 and 74.
9. 13, p. 158.
10. 13, p. 316.
11. 10, p. 377.
12. 1, p. 141.
13. 13, p. 548.
14. 14, p. 460.
15. Claude de Thiard de Bissy, *Histoire d'Ema*, 2 vols., Paris, 1752.
16. See B. F. Bart and Richard Francis Cook, *The Legendary Sources of Flaubert's 'Saint Julien'*, Toronto, 1977.
17. 13, p. 314.
18. 10, p. 44.
19. *Œuvres*, vol. II, p. 445.
20. *'Madame Bovary', Nouvelle Version*, p. 155.
21. 13, pp. 300–6.
22. *Contes*, ed. G. Rouger, Paris, 1967, pp. 3–10.
23. *'Madame Bovary', Nouvelle Version*, p. 525.
24. *De la religion considérée dans sa source, ses formes et ses développements*, 5 vols., 1824–30.
25. *Œuvres*, vol. II, p. 448.
26. 13, p. 661.
27. 4, 274.

28. 4, p. 424.
29. 10. p. 138.
30. 13, p. 178.
31. 10, p. 105.
32. *Isis* (first published 1845), in *Œuvres,* vol. I, pp. 324–8.
33. 13, p. 285.
34. 13, p. 314.
35. 14, p. 40.
36. 13, p. 214.
37. 13, p. 215.
38. 14, p. 386.
39. 13, p. 185.
40. 13, p. 570.
41. 12, p. 232.
42. 14, p. 20.
43. 13, p. 655.
44. 14, p. 20.
45. 13, p. 402.
46. See Margaret Lowe, ' "Rendre plastique . . .": Flaubert's Treatment of the Female Principle in *Hérodias', Modern Language Review,* July 1983.
47. 13, p. 181.
48. *Œuvres,* vol. II, p. 447.
49. *The Novels of Flaubert,* pp. 87–8.
50. 13, p. 675.

Chapter Three

1. *Essais,* p. 312.
2. *Les Fées du moyen âge, recherches sur leur origine, leur histoire et leurs attributs, pour servir à la connaissance de la mythologie gauloise.* Paris, 1843, and *La Normandie romanesque et merveilleuse. Traditions, légendes et superstitions de cette province,* Paris, 1845.
3. In *La Maison du berger.*
4. 13, p. 221.
5. *Traité du poème épique,* several times reprinted.
6. 13, p. 166.
7. *Œuvres posthumes,* Paris, 1939, vol. I, p. 240.
8. *Préface de Cromwell,* p. 211.
9. 13, p. 174.
10. 13, p. 178.
11. 13, p. 404.
12. 1, p. 453.
13. *'Madame Bovary', Nouvelle Version,* p. 170.
14. 6, p. 560.
15. 13, p. 422: 'Le temps n'est pas plus pur que le fond de mon cœur.'
16. 13, p. 445.
17. 12, p. 482.
18. 12, p. 534.
19. Ibid.
20. 12, p. 468.
21. 10, p. 434.

22. 10, p. 434.
23. 13, p. 365.
24. 13, p. 314.
25. 13, p. 399.
26. 13, p. 333.
27. Charles-François Dupuis, whose *Origines de tous les cultes, ou Religion universelle,* first published in 1795, was reprinted many times.
28. *Adolphe,* ed. J.-H. Bornecque, Paris, 1968, p. 137.
29. 11, p. 162.
30. 1, p. 549.
31. 1, p. 438.
32. *Commentaire sur 'Madame Bovary',* Neuchâtel, 1951, p. 44.
33. *'Madame Bovary', Nouvelle Version,* p. 140.
34. 13, p. 483.
35. *Œuvres,* vol. II, p. 449.
36. 13, p. 250.
37. 13, p. 315.

Chapter Four

1. 13, p. 272.
2. 13, p. 275.
3. 13, p. 271.
4. 13, p. 344.
5. 13, p. 247.
6. 13, p. 206.
7. 13, p. 393.
8. 12, p. 470.
9. 13, p. 233.
10. 11, p. 24.
11. 14, p. 466.
12. 13, p. 464.
13. 13, p. 361.
14. 1, p. 444.
15. In his article in *Le Moniteur universel,* 4 May 1857.
16. Paris, 1940.
17. *Littérature et sensation,* Paris, 1954.
18. *L'Expression figurée et symbolique dans l'œuvre de Gustave Flaubert,* Paris, 1931.
19. *Commentaire sur 'Madame Bovary',* p. 19.
20. *The Novels of Flaubert,* p. 148.
21. 13, p. 166.
22. 14, p. 66.
23. 13, p. 294.
24. 12, p. 49.
25. 14, p. 353.
26. 11, pp. 119 and 120.
27. 8, p. 287.
28. Quoted by Pierre Moreau, 'De la symbolique religieuse à la poésie symboliste', *Comparative Literature Studies,* IV, 1 and 2, 1967.
29. 12, p. 461.
30. 13, p. 233.

31. 13, p. 536.
32. 13, p. 419.
33. 13, p. 459.
34. 13, p. 384.
35. 14, p. 201.
36. 13, p. 268.
37. *L'Expression figurée et symbolique dans l'œuvre de Gustave Flaubert,* p. 458.
38. *'Madame Bovary', Nouvelle Version,* p. 599.
39. Ibid., p. 530.
40. 11, p. 654.
41. 2, p. 192.
42. 1, p. 438.
43. 4, p. 139.
44. 4, p. 136.
45. 13, p. 464.
46. 4, p. 66.
47. 1, p. 437.
48. 4, p. 132.
49. *'Madame Bovary', Nouvelle Version,* p. 48.
50. 13, p. 221.
51. 14, p. 85.
52. *Poésies,* Paris, 1950, p. 67.
53. 13, p. 362.
54. 9, pp. 275 and 420.

Chapter Five

1. Baudelaire, *L'Art philosophique* in *Œuvres,* vol. II, p. 370.
2. 9, p. 262.
3. *'Madame Bovary', Nouvelle Version,* p. 155.
4. 9, p. 275.
5. 13, p. 187.
6. 2, p. 53.
7. *Commentaire sur 'Madame Bovary',* p. 512.
8. 'The Role of Minerva in *Madame Bovary', Romance Notes,* VI, 2, 1965.
9. 13, pp. 410 and 416–7.
10. 13, p. 77.
11. 13, p. 214.
12. 13, p. 383.
13. *'Madame Bovary', Nouvelle Version,* p. 194.
14. 4, p. 437.
15. *'Madame Bovary', Nouvelle Version,* p. 332.
16. *Voyage en enfer* (not in the Club de l'Honnête Homme edition; see *Œuvres complètes,* ed. B. Masson, Paris, 1964, vol. I, p. 42).
17. 13, p. 545.
18. 14, p. 11.
19. Rabelais, Prologue to *Gargantua.* Part of this chapter has been adapted from 'Emma Bovary, a Modern Arachne', with the kind permission of the Editorial Board of *French Studies.*

Chapter Six

1. 9, p. 85.
2. *Les Fées du moyen âge, recherches sur leur origine, leur histoire et leurs attributs*, p. 4.
3. 10, p. 544.
4. 11, p. 448.
5. 13, p. 284.
6. 1, p. 539.
7. *'Madame Bovary', Nouvelle Version*, p. 17.
8. *Flaubert: 'Madame Bovary'*, London, 1962.
9. 2, p. 75.
10. 13, p. 501.
11. In *Madame Bovary*, Paris, 1930, p. 491.
12. 11, p. 436.
13. 11, p. 446.
14. *Essai historique, philosophique et pittoresque sur les danses des morts*, Rouen, 1851.
15. *Les Danses des morts, dissertations et recherches historiques, philosophiques, littéraires et musicales*, Paris, 1852.
16. Edmond and Jules de Goncourt, *Journal*, ed. R. Ricatte, Paris, 1956, vol. I, p. 308.
17. 14, p. 325.
18. 13, p. 498.
19. *'Madame Bovary', Nouvelle Version*, p. 117.
20. 11, p. 137.
21. 13, p. 302.
22. See Graham Daniels, 'Emma Bovary's Opera—Flaubert, Scott and Donizetti', *French Studies*, July 1978.
23. 11, p. 437.
24. 10, p. 509.
25. *Sensations et objets dans le roman de Flaubert*, Paris, 1973, pp. 289–90.

Publications by Margaret Lowe on Flaubert

'Flaubert's *Hérodias*—a New Evaluation' (with Colin Burns), *Montjoie,* vol. I, no. 1, May 1953.

'Emma Bovary, a Modern Arachne', *French Studies,* vol. XXVI, no 1, January 1972.

'Flaubert's *Hérodias,* "roman du Second Empire" ', *French Studies Bulletin,* no. 1, Winter 1981/2.

'*Hérodias,* the Second Empire and "la tête d'Orphée" ', *French Studies Bulletin,* no. 3, Summer 1982.

' "Rendre plastique . . ": Flaubert's Treatment of the Female Principle in *Hérodias', Modern Language Review,* vol. 78, no. 3, July 1983.

'Une vision ironique—*Hérodias'* in *Flaubert im Orient,* Frankfurt, Suhrkamp, forthcoming.

Bibliography

This bibliography has been compiled from Margaret Lowe's papers, but, as she did not prepare it herself, it can have no pretensions to completeness: she would certainly have wished to include other works which she considered relevant. Nevertheless, it should prove valuable even in its lacunary state.

The first section comprises books and articles on mythology and cognate topics which Flaubert himself either knew or might have known. Standard classics, whether Greek, Latin, or French, have been omitted; their inclusion would have lengthened the list to no good purpose.

The second section contains works on Flaubert quoted or consulted in the writing of the book. It is restricted to those items expressly mentioned in the text or in Dr Lowe's manuscript notes; short of giving an exhaustive Flaubert bibliography, which would have been impossibly bulky, it would have been arbitrary to go beyond that.

The final section consists of other modern studies, mainly on mythology and literature, used by Dr Lowe.

I

Baillet, A, *Les Vies des saints*, Paris, 1701–3.

Ballanche, P.-S., *Essais de Palingénésie sociale: prolégomènes, Orphée*, Paris, 1827–9.

Baudelaire, C., Review of *Prométhée délivré, Le Corsaire-Satan*, 3 février 1846 (also in *Œuvres*, Paris, 1938).

Bonneville, N. de, *De l'esprit des religions*, Paris, 1791.

Bosquet, A, *La Normandie romanesque et merveilleuse. Traditions, légendes et superstitions de cette province*, Paris, 1845.

Bouilhet, L, *Dernières Chansons* (préface de Gustave Flaubert), Paris, 1872.

Boulanger, N.-A., *L'Antiquité dévoilée par ses usages*, Amsterdam, 1766.

Buffon, G.-L. de, *Discours de l'Académie*, Paris, 1753.

Champollion-Figeac, J.-J., *L'Univers pittoresque: l'Égypte*, Paris, 1839.

Champollion le jeune, J.-F., *Lettres écrits d'Égypte et de Nubie en 1808*, Paris, 1833.

—— *Monuments de l'Égypte et de la Nubie*, Paris, 1835–72.

Chateaubriand, F.-R. de, *Le Génie du christianisme*, Paris, 1802.

Chénier, A, *Poésies*, Paris, 1819.

Chéruel, A., *Histoire de Rouen sous la domination anglaise au XVe siècle*, Rouen, 1840.

Chesneau, E., *Peinture, sculpture. Les nations rivales dans l'art*, Paris, 1868.

Colet, L., *Poésies complètes*, Paris, 1853.

Colet, L., *Le Poème de la femme*, Paris, 1853.

Constant, A.-L., *Assomption de la femme ou le livre de l'amour. Dogmes religieux et sociaux*, Paris, 1841.

—— *La Dernière Incarnation, légendes évangéliques*, Paris, 1841.

—— *La Clef des grands mystères*, Paris, 1861.

Constant, B., *Adolphe*, Paris, 1816 (also ed. J.-H. Bornecque, Paris, 1968).

—— *De la religion considérée dans sa source, ses formes et ses développements*, Paris, 1824–30.

Court de Gébelin, A., *Le Monde primitif analysé et comparé avec le monde moderne* (particularly Tome IV, *Le Monde primitif considéré dans l'histoire civile, religieuse et allégorique du calendrier ou almanach)*, Paris, 1773–82.

Cousin, V., *Cours de philosophie, professé à la Faculté de Lettres pendant l'année 1818 sur le fondement des idées absolues du Vrai, du Beau et du Bien*, Paris, 1837.

—— *Cours d'histoire de la philosophie morale au dix-huitième siècle professé en 1819 et 1820*, Paris, 1839–42.

Cox, G., *Les Dieux et les héros, contes mythologiques*, traduit par F. Baudry et E. Delerot, Paris 1867.

Creuzer, F., *Symbolik*, 1811–12, traduit par J.-D. Guignault sous le titre *Les Religions de l'antiquité considérées particulièrement sous leurs formes symboliques et mythologiques*, Paris, 1825–51.

Déal, J.-N., *Dissertation sur les Parisii ou Parisiens et sur le culte d'Isis chez les Gaulois*, Paris, 1826.

Delambre, J.-P.-J., *Histoire de l'astronomie ancienne*, Paris, 1817.

Douce, F., *The Dance of Death*, London, 1833.

Du Bois, L., *Préjugés et superstitions en Normandie*, Paris, 1843.

Dupuis, C.-F., *Origines de tous les cultes, ou Religion universelle*, Paris, 1795.

Flourens, P.-M.-J., *De la vie et de l'intelligence*, Paris, 1858.

Gassier, J.-M., *Histoire de la chevalerie française*, Paris, 1814.

Gautier, T., *Les Grotesques*, Paris, 1834–6.

—— *Le Roman de la momie*, Paris, 1858.

Gobineau, J.-A. de, *Essai sur l'inégalité des races humaines*, Paris, 1853–5.

Grimm, J. and W., *Les Veillées allemandes, chroniques, contes, traditions et croyances populaires*, Paris, 1838.

Gubernatis, A. de, *La Mythologie des plantes*, Paris, 1878–82.

Guignault, J.-D., *Le Dieu Sérapis et son origine, ses rapports, ses attributs et son histoire*, addition to Vol. III of Creuzer (q.v.), Paris, 1843.

—— *La Mythologie considérée dans ses principes, dans ses éléments et dans son histoire*, Paris, 1843.

(See also under Maury.)

Hugo, V., *Préface de Cromwell*, Paris, 1827 (new edition by M. Souriau, Paris, n.d.).

—— *Notre-Dame de Paris*, Paris, 1831.

—— *La Légende des siècles*, Paris, 1859–83.

Jacobi, E., *Dictionnaire mythologique universel*, traduit par T. Bernard, Paris, 1863.

Kastner, G., *Les Danses des morts, dissertations et recherches historiques, philosophiques, littéraires et musicales*, Paris, 1852.

Lamartine, A. de, *Voyage en Orient*, Paris, 1835.

—— *Jocelyn* (subtitle *Psyché*), Paris, 1836.

—— *La Chute d'un ange*, Paris, 1838.

—— *Graziella*, Paris, 1852.

Langlois, E.-H., *Mémoire sur la peinture sur verre et sur quelques vitraux remarquables des églises de Rouen*, Rouen, 1832.

—— *Essai historique et descriptif sur la peinture sur verre*, Rouen, 1832.

—— *Essai historique, philosophique et pittoresque sur les danses des morts*, Rouen, 1851.

Laprade, V. de, *Psyché*, Paris, 1841.

Le Bossu, Abbé, *Traité du poème épique*, Paris, 1675.

Leconte de Lisle, C., *Poèmes barbares*, Paris, 1852.

—— *Poèmes antiques*, Paris, 1862.

Macpherson, J., *The Poems of Ossian*, London, 1803.

Maury, A., *Essai sur les légendes pieuses au moyen âge*, Paris, 1843.

—— *Les Fées du moyen âge, recherches sur leur origine, leur histoire et leurs attributs, pour servir à la connaissance de la mythologie gauloise*, Paris, 1843.

—— *De l'hallucination envisagée au point de vue philosophique et historique*, Paris, 1845.

—— *Quelques observations sur le mythe du lion de Némée*, Paris, 1846.

—— *Des hallucinations hypnagogiques*, Paris, 1848.

—— *Histoire des religions de la Grèce antique*, Paris, 1857.

—— *Fragment d'un mémoire sur l'histoire de l'astrologie et de la magie dans l'antiquité et au Moyen Age*, Paris, 1859.

—— *Croyances et légendes de l'antiquité*, Paris, 1863.

—— *Les Ligures et l'arrivée des populations celtiques au Midi de la Gaule et en Espagne*, Paris, 1878.

—— et Guignault, J.-D., *La Nouvelle Galerie mythologique*, Paris, 1850.

—— et Pelletan, E., *Religions de l'Inde*, Paris, 1845.

Ménard, L., *Prométhée délivré*, Paris, 1843.

—— *Hermès Trismégiste, précédé d'une étude sur l'origine des livres hermétiques*, Paris, 1866.

—— *Étude sur les origines du Christianisme*, Paris, 1868.

Michelet, J., *Histoire romaine*, Paris, 1833.

Montaigne, M. de, *Essais*, Paris, 1950.

Müller, F. M., *Essais de mythologie comparée* (préface d'Ernest Renan), Paris, 1859.

—— *Origine et développement de la religion étudiés à la lumière des religions de l'Inde*, traduit par J. Parmesteter, Paris, 1879.

Müller, O., *De la poésie épique avant Homère et des œuvres d'Homère*, traduit par L. de Bouillé, Paris, 1846.

Nerval, G. de, *Voyage en Orient*, Paris, 1852 (also in *Œuvres*, ed. A. Béguin et J. Richer, Paris, 1956).

Ozanam, F., *Les Germains avant le Christianisme*, Paris, 1847.

Parny, E.-D. de, *Œuvres*, Paris, 1808.

Pelloutier, S., *Histoire des Celtes*, Paris, 1741.
Perrault, C., *Contes*, Paris, 1781 (also ed. G. Rouger, Paris, 1976).
Plancy, J.-A.-S. Collin de, *Les Fabliaux du Moyen Age*, Paris, 1846.
Portal, F., *Les Symboles des Égyptiens comparés à ceux des Hébreux*, Paris, 1840.
—— *Des couleurs symboliques dans l'antiquité, le Moyen Age et les temps modernes*, Paris, 1837.
Quinet, E., *Ahasvérus*, Paris, 1834.
Renan, E., *Vie de Jésus*, Paris, 1863.
—— *Histoire des origines du Christianisme*, Paris, 1863–83.
—— *L'Antéchrist*, Paris, 1873.
—— *Dialogues et fragments philosophiques*, Paris, 1876.
—— *Souvenirs d'enfance et de jeunesse*, Paris, 1883 (new edition 1953).
Sainte-Beuve, C.-A., *Tableau historique et critique de la poésie française et du théâtre français au seizième siècle*, Paris, 1828.
Saulcy, F. de, *Histoire de l'art judaïque*, Paris, 1858.
Scott, Sir W., *La Fiancée de Lammermoor* in *Œuvres*, traduites par Defau-compret, Paris, 1830–2.
—— *Lucia di Lammermoor* (opera by Donizetti), traduit par Royer et Vaëz.
Staël, Mme de, *Delphine*, Paris, 1802.
—— *Corinne*, Paris, 1807.
Taine, H., *De l'idéal dans l'art*, Paris, 1867.
Thiard de Bissy, C. de, *Histoire d'Ema*, Paris, 1752.
Thierry, J-N.-A., *Histoire des Gaulois*, Paris, 1828.
—— *Récits des temps mérovingiens précédés de considérations sur l'histoire de la France*, Paris, 1840.
Vigny, A. de, *Les Destinées*, Paris, 1846.
Villemain, A.-F. de, *Cours de littérature française du Moyen Age*, Paris, 1830.
Volney, C.-F., *Œuvres choisies*, Paris, 1827.
Voragine, J. de, *La Légende dorée*, traduite par J. de Vignay, Paris, 1832.
Walckenaer, C.-A., *Lettres sur les contes de fées attribués à Perrault et sur l'origine de la féerie*, Paris, 1826.
Wilkinson, G., *Manners and Customs of the Ancient Egyptians*, London, 1837.
Winckelmann, J., *De l'allégorie*, traduit par H. Jansen (?), Paris, n.d.

II

Albalat, A., *Gustave Flaubert et ses amis*, Paris, 1927.
Barbey d'Aurevilly, J., Review of *L'Éducation sentimentale*, *Le Constitutionnel*, 19 décembre 1869.
—— 'Gustave Flaubert' in *Le Roman contemporain*, Paris, 1902.
Barnes, H. E., *Sartre and Flaubert*, Chicago, 1981.
Bart, B. F., *Madame Bovary and the Critics*, New York, 1966.
—— *Flaubert*, Syracuse, 1967.
—— and Cook, R. F., *The Legendary Sources of Flaubert's 'Saint Julien'*, Toronto, 1977.

Baudelaire, C., 'Gustave Flaubert, *Madame Bovary, La Tentation de Saint Antoine*', *L'Artiste*, 18 oct. 1857 (also in *Œuvres,* Paris, 1938).

Bem, J., *Désir et savoir dans l'œuvre de Flaubert: étude de 'La Tentation de Saint Antoine'*, Neuchâtel and Paris, 1979.

Benedetto, L. F., *Le Origini di 'Salammbô': Studio sul realismo storico di Gustave Flaubert*, Florence, 1920.

Bertrand, L., 'Les Carnets inédits de Flaubert', *Revue des Deux Mondes,* juillet 1910.

—— *Gustave Flaubert, avec des fragments inédits,* Paris, 1912.

Bismut, R., 'Sur une chronologie de *Madame Bovary*', *Amis de Flaubert,* mai 1973.

Blossom, F. A., *La Composition de 'Salammbô',* New York, 1914.

Bopp, L., *Commentaire sur 'Madame Bovary',* Neuchatel, 1951.

Brombert, V., *The Novels of Flaubert,* Princeton, 1966.

—— *Flaubert par lui-même,* Paris, 1971.

Brown, D. F., 'The Veil of Tanit: the personal significance of a woman's adornment to Gustave Flaubert', *Romanic Review,* 1943.

Bruneau, J., *Les Débuts littéraires de Gustave Flaubert (1830–1845),* Paris, 1962.

—— 'Les Deux Voyages de Gustave Flaubert en Italie' in *Mélanges offerts à J.-M. Carré,* Paris, 1964.

—— 'Le Rôle du hasard dans *L'Éducation sentimentale*', *Europe,* sept.–oct.–nov. 1969.

—— *Le 'Conte oriental' de Flaubert,* Paris, 1973.

—— (ed.), Flaubert, *Correspondance,* Paris, Vol. I, 1973, Vol. II, 1980 (in progress).

Cannon, J. H., 'L'Esthétique de Flaubert d'après *Hérodias*', unpublished M.A. thesis, Manchester University, 1952.

—— 'Flaubert's documentation for *Hérodias*', *French Studies,* October 1960.

Carlut, C., Dubé, P. H. and Dugan, J. R., *A Concordance to Flaubert's 'Madame Bovary',* New York and London, 1978.

Castex, P.-G., 'Bibliothèque de *L'Éducation sentimentale*', *L'Information littéraire,* octobre 1980.

—— *Flaubert: 'L'Éducation sentimentale',* Paris, 1980.

Cellier, L., '*L'Éducation sentimentale*', in *Études de structure,* Paris, 1964.

Chevalley-Sabatier, L., *Gustave Flaubert et sa nièce Caroline,* Paris, 1971.

Cigada, S., 'Genesi e struttura tematica di *Madame Bovary*', *Contributi del Seminario di Filologia moderna,* Milan, 1959.

Cogny, P., '*L'Éducation sentimentale' de Flaubert: le monde en creux,* Paris, 1975.

Commanville, C., 'Souvenirs intimes' in *Correspondance de Gustave Flaubert,* Paris, 1887.

Cross, R. K., *Flaubert and Joyce. The Rite of Fiction,* Princeton, 1971.

Crouzet, M., 'Le Style épique dans *Madame Bovary*', *Europe,* sept.–oct.–nov. 1969.

Daniels, G., 'Emma Bovary's Opera—Flaubert, Scott and Donizetti', *French Studies,* July 1978.

Danger, P., *Sensations et objets dans le roman de Flaubert*, Paris, 1973.
Danner, L., 'Poetic Symbolism in *Madame Bovary*', *Fourth Atlantic Quarterly*, April 1956.
Debray-Genette, R., 'Flaubert: science et écriture', *Littérature*, octobre 1974.
—— 'Re-présentation d'*Hérodias*' in *Là Production du sens chez Flaubert*, Paris, 1975.
Degoumois, L., *Flaubert à l'école de Goethe*, Genève, 1925.
Demorest, D. L., *L'Expression figurée et symbolique dans l'œuvre de Gustave Flaubert*, Paris, 1931.
—— and Dumesnil, R., *Bibliographie de Gustave Flaubert*, Paris, 1931.
Diamond, M. J., *Flaubert: the Problem of Aesthetic Discontinuity*, New York and London, 1975.
Digeon, C., *Le Dernier Visage de Flaubert*, Paris, 1946.
—— *Flaubert*, Paris, 1970.
Douchin, J.-L., *Le Sentiment de l'absurde chez Gustave Flaubert*, Paris, 1970.
Duchet, C., 'Roman et objets, l'exemple de *Madame Bovary*', *Europe*, sept.-oct.-nov. 1969.
Dumesnil, R., *'Madame Bovary' de Gustave Flaubert*, Paris, 1940.
—— *'L'Éducation sentimentale' de Gustave Flaubert*, Paris, 1943.
—— 'Les Sources de *Salammbô*', *Revue des Deux Mondes*, LXXIV, 1943.
—— *Flaubert: Documents iconographiques*, Geneva, 1948.
—— *Gustave Flaubert: l'homme et l'œuvre*, Paris, 1967.
—— and Descharmes, R.: *Autour de Flaubert*, Paris, 1912.
Durry, M.-J., *Flaubert et ses projets inédits*, Paris, 1950.
Fairlie, A., *Flaubert: 'Madame Bovary'*, London, 1962.
—— 'Flaubert et la conscience du réel', *Essays in French Literature*, Nov. 1967.
—— 'Flaubert and Some Painters of his Time' in *The Artist and the Writer in France—Essays in Honour of Jean Seznec*, Oxford, 1974.
Fay, P. B., and Coleman, A., *Sources and Structures of Flaubert's 'Salammbô'*, New York, 1914.
Genette, G., 'Le Travail de Flaubert', *Tel Quel*, été 1963.
—— 'Silences de Flaubert' in *Figures I*, Paris, 1969.
Giraud, R., 'La Genèse d'un chef-d'œuvre: *La Légende de saint Julien l'Hospitalier*', *Revue Nouvelle des Lettres Françaises*, janv.-mars 1919.
Goncourt, E. and J. de, *Journal*, ed. R. Ricatte, Paris, 1956.
Gothot-Mersch, C., *La Genèse de 'Madame Bovary'*, Paris, 1966.
Grant, R. B., 'The Role of Minerva in *Madame Bovary*', *Romance Notes*, VI, 2, 1965.
Grappin, H., 'Le mysticisme et l'imagination de Flaubert', *Revue de Paris*, décembre 1912.
Green, A., '*Salammbô* and the Myth of Pasiphaë', *French Studies*, April 1978.
—— *Flaubert and the Historical Novel: 'Salammbô' Reassessed*, Cambridge, 1982.

Hamilton, A., *Sources of the Religious Element in Flaubert's 'Salammbô'*, New York and Paris, 1917.

Huss, R., 'Nature, Final Causality and Anthropomorphism in Flaubert', *French Studies*, July 1979.

Jacobs, A. (ed.), *Correspondance Flaubert–Sand*, Paris, 1981.

Jasinski, R., 'Le Sens des *Trois Contes*' in *Essays in honour of L. F. Solano*, North Carolina, 1970.

Lapp, J. C., 'Art and Hallucination in Flaubert', *French Studies*, October 1956.

La Varende, J. de, *Flaubert par lui-même*, Paris, 1951.

Leleu, G., '*Madame Bovary*'. *Ébauches et fragments inédits*, Paris, 1936.

Lombard, A., *Flaubert et saint Antoine*, Paris, 1934.

Maupassant, G. de, 'Étude sur Gustave Flaubert' in *Correspondance entre George Sand et Flaubert*, Paris, 1884.

Mauriac, F., *Trois Grands Hommes devant Dieu: Molière, Rousseau, Flaubert*, Paris, 1947.

Mayoux, J.-J. 'Flaubert et le réel', *Mercure de France*, février 1934.

Nadeau, M., *Gustave Flaubert écrivain*, Paris, 1969.

Neefs, J., '*Madame Bovary*', Paris, 1972.

Oliver, H., *Flaubert and an English Governess*, Oxford, 1980.

Pommier, J., 'Noms et prénoms dans *Madame Bovary*', *Mercure de France*, juin 1949.

—— and Digeon, C., 'Du nouveau sur Flaubert et son œuvre', *Mercure de France*, mai 1952.

—— and Leleu, G., '*Madame Bovary*', *Nouvelle Version*, Paris, 1949.

Proust, J., 'Structure et sens de *L'Éducation sentimentale*', *Revue des Sciences Humaines*, janv.-mars 1967.

Proust, M., 'A propos du style de Flaubert' in *Œuvres complètes*, Paris, 1936.

Raitt, A. W., 'The Composition of Flaubert's *Saint Julien l'Hospitalier*', *French Studies*, October 1965.

Richard, J.-P., *Littérature et sensation*, Paris, 1954.

Robertson, J., 'The Structure of *Hérodias*', *French Studies*, April 1982.

Sainte-Beuve, C.-A., '*Madame Bovary* de Gustave Flaubert', *Le Moniteur Universel*, 10 mai 1857.

Sartre, J.-P., *L'Idiot de la famille*, Paris, 1971–2.

Seebacher, J., 'Le Réalisme de *Bouvard et Pécuchet*: notes pour une topographie utopique', *Cahiers de recherche de S.T.D.*, automne 1970.

Seznec, J., *Les Sources de l'épisode des dieux dans 'La Tentation de saint Antoine'*, Paris, 1940.

—— 'Saint Antoine et les monstres', *Publications of the Modern Language Association of America*, March 1943.

—— 'Flaubert historien des hérésies dans *La Tentation*', *Romanic Review*, Oct.–Dec. 1945.

—— *Nouvelles Études sur 'La Tentation de saint Antoine'*, London, 1949.

—— *Flaubert à l'Exposition de 1851*, Oxford, 1951.

Sherrington, R. J., *Three Novels by Flaubert: a Study of Techniques*, Oxford, 1970.

Starkie, E., *Flaubert. The Making of the Master,* London, 1967.
—— *Flaubert. The Master,* London, 1971.
Steegmuller, F., *Flaubert and Madame Bovary: a Double Portrait,* London, 1947.
Suhner-Schluep, F., *L'Imagination du feu ou la dialectique du soleil et de la lune dans 'Salammbô',* Zurich, 1970.
Thibaudet, A., *Gustave Flaubert,* Paris, 1935.
Thorlby, A., *Gustave Flaubert and the Art of Realism,* London, 1956.
Tooke, A., 'A Study of Flaubert's *Par les champs et par les grèves',* unpublished Ph. D. thesis, Cambridge University, 1977.
Unwin, T. A., *Flaubert et Baudelaire: affinités spirituelles et esthétiques,* Paris, 1982.
Valéry, P., 'La Tentation de (saint) Flaubert' in *Œuvres,* Vol. I, Paris, 1962.
Weck, R. de, 'L'Ascétisme de Flaubert', *Mercure de France,* mai 1930.
Weil, A., 'Le Style de *Salammbô',* *Revue universitaire,* avril 1902.
Wetherill, P. M., *Flaubert et la création littéraire,* Paris, 1964.
—— (ed.), *Flaubert: la dimension du texte,* Manchester, 1982.
Willenbrink, G., *The Dossier of Flaubert's 'Un Cœur simple',* Amsterdam, 1976.
Williams, D. A., *Psychological Determinism in 'Madame Bovary',* Hull, 1973.
Zola, É., 'Gustave Flaubert' in *Les Romanciers naturalistes,* Paris, 1895.

III

.

Auerbach, E., *Mimesis,* translated by W. R. Trask, Princeton, 1968.
Bachelard, G., *L'Eau et les rêves,* Paris, 1940.
Bell, H. J., *Cults and Creeds in Greco-Roman Egypt,* Liverpool, 1953.
Belmont, N., *Mythes et croyances dans l'ancienne France,* Paris, 1973.
Bodkin, M., *Archetypal Patterns in Poetry,* London, 1948.
Bouquet, F., *Discours sur l'histoire de l'enseignement supérieur à Rouen pendant le XIXe siècle 1808–1896,* Rouen, 1896.
Buffière, F., *Les Mythes d'Homère et la pensée grecque,* Paris, 1956.
Cabrol, Dom, et Leclercq, Dom, *Dictionnaire d'archéologie chrétienne et de liturgie,* Paris, 1939–40.
Cassirer, E., *An Essay on Man,* New Haven, 1944.
—— *Language and Myth,* translated by S. K. Langer, New York, 1946.
—— *The Philosophy of Symbolic Forms,* translated by R. Manheim, New Haven, 1953–7.
Castor, G., *Pléiade Poetics: a Study in Sixteenth-Century Thought and Terminology,* Cambridge, 1964.
Cellier, L., 'Le Romantisme et le mythe d'Orphée', *Cahiers de l'Association Internationale des Études françaises,* 1958.
Charbonneau-Lassay, L., *Le Bestiaire du Christ,* Milan, 1940.
Chevallier, J., and Gheerbrant, A., *Dictionnaire des symboles,* Paris, 1969.
Clark, R., and Rundle, T., *Myth and Symbol in Ancient Egypt,* London, 1959.

Cooper, W. R., *The Horus Myth in its Relation to Christianity*, London, 1959.

Coulson, J. (ed.), *Dictionnaire historique des saints*, traduit par B. Noël, Paris, 1964.

Damon, P., *Modes of Analogy in Ancient Egypt and Medieval Verse*, Berkeley, 1961.

Delcourt, M., *Hermaphrodite: mythes et rites de la bisexualité dans l'antiquité classique*, Paris, 1958.

Demerson, G., *La Mythologie classique dans l'œuvre de la Pléiade*, Genève, 1972.

Dennis, J. T., *The Burden of Isis, being the Laments of Isis and Nephthys*, London, 1910.

Diel, P., *Le Symbolisme dans la mythologie grecque*, Paris, 1966.

Dill, S. *Roman Society from Nero to Marcus Aurelius*, London and New York, 1964.

Doresse, J., *The Secret Book of the Ancient Gnostics*, London, 1960.

Durry, M.-J., *Gérard de Nerval et le mythe*, Paris, 1956.

Fairlie, A., *Leconte de Lisle's Poems on the Barbarian Races*, Cambridge, 1947.

Festugière, A.-J., *La Philosophie de l'amour de Marsile Ficin et son influence*, Paris, 1941.

Flacelière, R., *L'Amour en Grèce*, Paris, 1960.

Gatinsky, G. K., *The Herakles Theme. The Adaptation of the Hero in Literature from Homer to the Twentieth Century*, Ottowa, 1972.

Graillot, H., *Le Culte de Cybèle, mère des dieux*, Paris, 1912.

Graves, R., *The Greek Myths*, Harmondsworth, 1955.

—— *The White Goddess*, London, 1959.

Guthrie, W. K. C., *Orpheus and Greek Religion*, London, 1950.

Harrison, J. E., *Prolegomena to the Study of Greek Religion*, Cambridge, 1903.

Hatch, E., *The Influence of Greek Ideas and Usages upon the Christian Church*, London, 1888.

Hunt, H. J., *The Epic in Nineteenth-Century France*, Oxford, 1941.

Jankélévitch, V., *L'Ironie*, Paris, 1964.

Jones, E., *The Life and Work of Sigmund Freud*, Harmondsworth, 1964.

Juden, B., *Traditions orphiques et tendances mystiques dans le romantisme français 1800–1855*, Paris, 1971.

Jung, C. J., and Kerenyi, K., *Introduction to a Science of Mythology: the Myth of the Divine Child and the Mysteries of Eleusis*, translated by R. F. C. Hull, London, 1951.

Kushner, E., *Le Mythe d'Orphée dans la littérature française*, Paris, 1961.

Lafaye, G., *Histoire du culte des divinités d'Alexandrie*, Paris, 1884.

Lecouteux, C., *Mélusine et le Chevalier au Cygne*, Paris, 1982.

Lemaître, H., *Essai sur le mythe de Psyché dans la littérature française*, Paris, 1946.

Marache, M., *Le Symbole dans la pensée et l'œuvre de Goethe*, Paris, 1960.

Merril, R. V., *Platonism in French Renaissance Poetry*, New York, 1957.

Mondor, H., *Vie de Mallarmé*, Paris, 1941.

Moreau, P., 'De la symbolique religieuse à la poésie symboliste', *Comparative Literature Studies*, IV, 1 and 2, 1967.

Murdoch, I., *The Fire and the Sun: Why Plato Banished the Artists*, Oxford, 1967.

Murray, G., *The Rise of the Greek Epic*, Oxford, 1911.

Nilsson, N. M., *A History of Greek Religion*, Oxford, 1925.

Ploix, C., *Mythologie et folklorisme: les mythes de Kronos et de Psyché*, Paris, 1886.

—— *La Nature et les dieux: études de mythologie gréco-latine*, Paris,1888.

Praz, M., *Mnemosyne. The Parallel between Literature and the Visual Arts*, Washington, 1970.

Przlinski, J., *La Grande Déesse*, Paris, 1950.

Renel, C., *Les Religions de la Gaule avant le Christianisme*, Paris, 1906.

Ribard, J., *La Chevalerie de la charrette, essai d'interprétation symbolique*, Paris, 1972.

Riffaterre, H. B., *L'Orphisme dans la poésie romantique*, Paris, 1970.

Richter, W., *Myth and Literature*, London, 1975.

Robert, F., *La Littérature grecque*, Paris, 1971.

Saintyves, P., *Les Contes de Perrault et leurs récits parallèles: leurs origines (coutumes primitives et liturgies populaires)*, Paris, 1923.

—— *Saint Christophe, successeur d'Anubis, d'Hermès et d'Héracles*, Paris, 1936.

Sartre, J.-P., *Critique de la raison dialectique*, Paris, 1960.

Seznec, J., *La Survivance des dieux antiques*, London, 1940.

Soriano, M., *Les Contes de Perrault, culture savante et tradition populaire*, Paris, 1968.

Strauss, W. A., *Descent and Return: the Orphic Theme in Modern Literature*, London, 1971.

Taillardat, J., *Les Images d'Aristophane*, Paris, 1902.

Valéry, P., 'La Jeune Parque' in *Poésies*, Paris, 1950.

Verneuil, P., *Dictionnaire des symboles, emblèmes et attributs*, Paris, 1897.

Williams, C., *The Figure of Beatrice*, London, 1943.

Witt, R. E., *Isis in the Graeco-Roman World*, London and Southampton, 1971.

Zumthor, P., *Histoire littéraire de la France médiévale, XIe–XIVe siècle*, Paris, 1954.

Index